THE SMART GUIDE TO AUTO LEASING

GREGORY STEWART

CB
CONTEMPORARY
BOOKS
CHICAGO

Library of Congress Cataloging-in-Publication Data

Stewart, Gregory.
    The smart guide to auto leasing / Gregory Stewart.
       p.   cm.
    Includes index.
    ISBN 0-8092-4110-2 (pbk.) : $7.95
    1. Automobiles, Rental.   I. Title.
HD9710.A2S85   1990
388.3'2—dc20   90-1967
                                                                    CIP

PUBLISHER'S NOTE:

The material contained in *The Smart Guide to Auto Leasing* is intended to present an overview of the advantages and mechanics of consumer and business auto leasing. One of the benefits of auto leasing involves certain tax advantages over other forms of financing. While *The Smart Guide to Auto Leasing* attempts to provide current tax information, the book is not intended as a substitute for qualified counsel.

While every attempt has been made to provide accurate information, neither the author nor the publisher can be held accountable for any error or omission.

Copyright © 1990 by Gregory Stewart
All rights reserved
Published by Contemporary Books, Inc.
180 North Michigan Avenue, Chicago, Illinois 60601
Manufactured in the United States of America
International Standard Book Number: 0-8092-4110-2

Contents

1 INTRODUCTION 1
   What Is a Lease?
   Closed-End and Open-End Leases
   Benefits of Leasing

2 TYPES OF LEASES 9
   Long-Term Leases
   Short-Term Leases
   Manufacturer's Leases

3 SPECIAL STRATEGIES 20
   High-Mileage Strategy
   Tax Strategies for Business Use
   Leasing to Buy

4 SHOPPING FOR A LEASE 33
   Figuring the Cost of a Lease
   Smilin' Sammy in the Lease Office
   Finding the Best Deal
   What to Look for in the Contract
     (Regulation M)

5 BUYING INSURANCE 60

6	**TERMINATING YOUR LEASE**	64
	At the End of the Lease Term	
	Getting Out of Your Lease Early	
	Buying Your Leased Car	
	Selling Your Car	
7	**ANSWERS TO YOUR QUESTIONS ON LEASING**	75
	GLOSSARY	82
	MONTHLY PAYMENT TABLES FOR CONVENTIONAL LOANS	86
	INDEX	98

1
Introduction

In the past few years, consumer leasing has become increasingly popular. Approximately 20 percent of the new cars leaving showroom floors are leased, and that number is predicted to grow to 50 percent. Perhaps a couple of your friends have leased, or maybe you've read about the benefits (and risks) of leasing in a magazine article.

What exactly is involved in leasing an auto? Why are so many people choosing to lease instead of buy? Reading this book will help you answer those questions. To the uninitiated, leasing may seem no more than "voodoo economics," but this book and its glossary of common terms will uncloak some of the mystery. Once you decide you want to lease, you'll be equipped to negotiate a leasing deal that meets your needs.

WHAT IS A LEASE?

A lease is a contract to rent something. When you sign a lease, you agree to pay some amount of money in exchange for the right to use the leased item.

Leasing a car is much like renting anything. If you have ever rented an apartment, for example, you probably made a security deposit. But you didn't have to make a down payment, as you would to take out a loan to buy a condo. Likewise, with an auto lease, there is no down payment, though you will have to put down the first month's rent and a refundable security deposit. Instead of paying the entire cost of the item, as you would if you were buying, you pay only for the value of using the car. As when you rent an apartment, though, at the end of the lease you'll end up with rent receipts instead of equity. In other words, you must return the car at the end of the lease; you have no ownership rights.

The monthly payments on an auto lease are based on the difference between the car's sales price and the value the car is expected to have at the end of the lease term. This value is called the *residual value* and is usually set when the contract is negotiated. So, for example, if a car's sales price is $20,000 and its residual value is established to be $5,000, the monthly payments are based on the difference, which is $15,000. In addition, you pay finance charges, just as you would if you were taking out a loan to buy the car. However, the interest rate for financing is generally set a percentage point or so lower than the prevailing interest rate on an auto loan. The monthly payment also includes a portion of the sales tax on the car.

An auto lease involves a variety of charges besides the monthly rental payments. Up front, you can expect to pay for licensing, registration, and other costs to the dealer—again, just as you would if you were buying the car. You'll have to pay the first month's rent, as well as a security deposit, which is usually equal to the first month's rent. When you turn in the car, it will be used to cover any damage over "average wear and tear." At the end of the lease, you will also have to pay for excess mileage on the car (usually 8 cents for each additional mile over 15,000 total miles per year on the car).

CLOSED-END AND OPEN-END LEASES

There are two general types of leases, closed-end and open-end. The more common of the two is the *closed-end lease*. With this type of lease, the lessee bears no responsibility for the car's resale value at lease-end (other than, again, for damage above average wear and tear and for excess mileage fees). If the car's market value at the end of the lease is lower than the residual set by the dealer at lease inception, the lease bank takes that loss, not you. You can turn in the car and walk away.

The alternative is an *open-end lease*. With this type of lease, you share in the risk that the car will not be worth the residual value at the end of the lease term. At lease-end, the fair market value of your car will be determined, most likely by a dealer's guide to current wholesale prices. If the car is worth at least as much as the residual, you may buy it for the price of the residual, knowing you got a good deal. However, if the car's determined market value is less than the residual value, you will be responsible for paying the difference. You can buy the car yourself by paying the residual value, but that means you will be paying more than the car is worth—such is the risk of open-end leases. Even though the high risk of these leases makes them less expensive than closed-end leases, they should be avoided. Open-end leases are rarely used for consumer leases today, and this book primarily discusses closed-end leases.

WHAT IS A LEASE?

- A lease is a contract to rent something, that is, to pay rent in exchange for being able to use something.
- With an auto lease, you pay only for the use of the car, plus certain fees, not the car's full price.
- Leases often involve no down payment.
- At the end of the lease, you will have no equity in the car.
- Leases can be closed-end or open-end.
- Closed-end leases are the preferable type for consumers

BENEFITS OF LEASING

Almost always, the first question an auto dealership's leasing manager hears from a customer is "Can leasing benefit me?"

In fact, leasing does offer a variety of benefits that apply to typical consumers.

Cash Flow

One of the main motives for leasing is that it reduces outward-bound cash flow. Most important, you'll have smaller monthly payments for a given car. Since a lessee pays only for the use of the car instead of for the entire car, payments often run 20–30 percent less than to purchase the car. This frees up cash for you to save or to spend elsewhere.

Leasing instead of buying also means paying less sales tax. Although this tax is computed differently from state to state (in some states the lessee is not even required to pay sales tax), most states require that sales tax be based not on the original purchase price, but on the difference between that and the residual price plus financing and other costs to the dealer. The tax is spread over the life of the lease, so the lessee pays only a few dollars of sales tax each month instead of several hundred dollars out of pocket right off the top, as you would if you were buying.

Also, remember that a lease does not require a down payment, which means you avoid the task of pooling several thousand dollars to get the car on the road. This benefit is especially helpful for a young couple looking for their first car or an established family requiring a second or third car—they don't need a trade-in car or a lot of cash to use toward a down payment.

Just as important, the cash that would have gone for a down payment can be put to more profitable uses. Leasing can really pay off when you take the money you would have used as a down payment and invest it in an interest-bearing account such as a money market fund or certificate of deposit. The $1,500 you might have used for a 10 percent down payment on a $15,000 car could be invested at say, 8 percent. If so, that money could earn $720 over four years. Investing money makes more sense economically than tying up cash in a depreciating asset like an automobile, which will only lose value over time.

Changes in Tax Benefits

These benefits to your cash flow are especially important today, when past tax benefits of purchasing are no longer available. In 1986 Congress enacted major changes to the tax law that affect the way we think about all major purchases, especially car purchases. Since 1987 the amount of sales tax we can deduct from gross income has dwindled each year—to zero after 1990. Likewise, after 1990, the interest paid on a car loan is no longer deductible. Since interest and sales taxes generally run more for buying, the main tax breaks for traditional financing are disappearing, making leasing relatively more attractive than it used to be.

Certainty of Resale

A growing segment of conservative people like the certainty of a lease. Closed-end leases guarantee the resale price of the car in advance, so when it comes time to turn in "Old Betsy," there's no haggling with used-car dealers over the trade-in value. At lease-end you can return the car and walk away. If the car depreciates more than anticipated, the lessor takes the loss, not you.

Fancier Car

The least practical justification for leasing, though still a genuine motive for many people, is that leasing allows them to drive a more expensive car than they could if they bought. A given monthly payment covers the leasing costs on a more expensive car than you could buy with the same outlay per month.

For example, if you want to pay no more than $300 per month for a new car, 10 percent down and a 9.5 percent interest rate for 48 months would purchase a $13,000 car.

(For payments at various interest rates and terms, see the monthly payment charts at the back of the book.) For the same monthly payment, you could easily lease a car costing several thousand dollars more.

Will *You* Benefit?—A Quiz

Not everyone benefits from leasing. Take this simple quiz to see if leasing is something that you should be looking into:

1. Will you put fewer than 15,000 miles per year on the car that you are currently seeking?
2. Will you want to sell this car by its fifth birthday?
3. Are you generally "kind" to your car, keeping it relatively damage-free?
4. Will you want to be out of this car by its third birthday?
5. Do you earn over $30,000 per year or approximately twice the list price of the car you are seeking (Whichever is higher)?
6. Do you have an established A1 credit rating?

If the answer to any of these questions is *no*, then you might want to reevaluate your decision to lease. You may wish to use the special strategies outlined in Chapter 3, or perhaps you would be better off to purchase.

After 15,000 miles per year, most lease contracts force you to pay a penalty. This penalty is generally 8 cents per mile, which can become costly over many miles. If you drive 17,000 miles one year and 13,000 miles the next, you are on track. It is the average that counts. If you consistently run many miles over the limit, read about short-term leases in Chapter 2 and about high-mileage strategy in Chapter 3.

If you are one of those people who want to keep a car until you plow it into the earth, you may still be better off leasing the car. It can be less expensive, and you can always change your mind about purchasing at the end of the lease. However, you will have to do some careful arithmetic to be sure that you are not getting stuck in a lease that is too expensive. Read the material on leasing to buy in Chapter 3.

If you are one of those people who use a car roughly and consider it mere transportation, be careful about leasing. The lease company will make a customer pay for any damages above "average wear and tear." If you decide to abort the lease, a worn car will diminish your chances of getting a fair price.

If you are certain to keep the car less than 48 months, you are probably a good lease customer, but some special strategies might help your position. Read the sections on short-term and manufacturer's leases in Chapter 2.

If you answered no to either of the last two questions, you may want to lease but may have a problem getting approved by a competitive bank. With leasing, the bank has no down payment to offset the initial depreciation of the automobile. Because automobiles are declining assets, the bank cannot recover 100 percent of its investment should you default in the first two years. For this reason, lenders are very particular about the people they approve for a lease contract.

Do the Math

When all is said and done, a lessee has no equity (a car) at the end of a lease. If you plan to drive the car for several years after it is paid off, this is an important consideration. However, if you, like many people, plan only to use the car as a trade-in on your next car, this "drawback" becomes less important. Something to keep in mind is that you *can* buy your car at the end of the lease (see the discussion of leasing to buy in Chapter 3 and the discussion of the fixed purchase option in Chapter 4's description of contract provisions). This means that you can either continue to drive the car or sell it, and if the car is worth more than the residual price in the lease, you can pocket the difference.

Potential lessees, then, must do the math carefully to make

sure leasing will pay off. Most important in deciding if leasing is right for you, of course, is to compute the rough difference between buying and leasing. Even if you are planning to buy your car at the end of your lease, the formulas on leasing to buy vs. purchasing in Chapter 3 will help you compare the costs of leasing to buying. (See the more detailed formula in the section on figuring the cost of a lease in Chapter 4, for more precise figures.)

Sometimes the difference between leasing and conventional financing is negligible. Many times the difference depends on whether you invest your down payment money, what the sales tax in your area is, and whether you avoid excess-mileage costs. The following chapter will give a formula to help in deciding whether leasing makes sense for you.

BENEFITS OF LEASING

- Monthly payments are generally smaller and fit more easily into a budget.
- Down payments are not required, making it unnecessary to save a pool of cash.
- The diminished tax benefits of purchasing no longer offset the financial benefits of leasing.
- With a closed-end lease, the resale value of the car is established at the start of the contract.
- The same monthly payment can go for a fancier car.
- The benefits from leasing depend upon each individual's financial status and plans for the car.
- Before deciding, compute the costs of buying and leasing.

2
Types of Leases

If you think an auto lease is a good idea for you, it's wise to consider the variety of leases that are available. Long-term and short-term leases offer different benefits. And in some cases, you may want to consider a manufacturer's lease.

LONG-TERM LEASES

Leasing has changed since the 1986 tax program eliminated the investment tax credit (ITC) from the warehouse of corporate deductions. Since this ITC was generally not passed on to the customer, the financing banks were able to draw upon this credit for their own purposes. It amounted to $750 per leased vehicle for all vehicles of $12,500 and over. This credit allowed the banks to be liberal with their residual values (the value for which the bank will own the car at lease-end). They could, after all, fall back upon the ITC if the resale value of the car fell short of its anticipated wholesale value. The banks do not have the ITC anymore, and residual values have fallen about $800 per car. There is no coincidence here. The banks protect themselves by figuring the value of their returning cars at a "worst-case scenario" and, in fact, have let the residuals drop below wholesale.

A long-term lease strategy was developed in order to take advantage of the lower residuals without paying for a bank's worst-case scenario. This strategy is a long-term, level-yield lease.

Long-term leases offer the least expensive way to get into a new car, as the monthly payments are smaller than for a shorter, conventional lease. With low residuals you achieve equity sooner (you'll see why in a moment), so you can buy out your lease after three, four, or five years without losing money. This gives you more flexibility than a conventional lease, which can be very expensive to terminate early. However, you must be certain to stay in the lease for at least three years—a long-term lease is very expensive to terminate early. Also, this long-term strategy should not be combined with any other strategy or plan, particularly the high-mileage strategy. If you are not planning to buy the car at the end of the term, will put no more than average mileage on the car (15,000–16,000 miles per year), and, again, plan to be in the lease for at least three years, it would benefit you to pursue this strategy.

The typical long-term auto lease spreads payments out over 60 months (five years). Long-term leases generally use conservative residual values. Be sure the dealer or lease bank is using ALG residuals—those based on the *ALG Residual Percentage Guide*, which sets residuals lower than market values. This is important if you buy out your lease before the term is up. In contrast to the payments on most leases, each monthly payment consists of the same proportion of interest and principal. This "level-yield" feature means that you are paying off the principal relatively quickly, so you achieve equity sooner. (Be sure your long-term lease includes this level-yield feature, as not all do.)

Certain lenders expect you to pay unearned interest and penalties if you terminate the lease early. This is not illegal in all states, but it is highly unethical. A top priority when considering any lease should be to look for the rules regarding early termination.

To see the benefits of a long-term lease, consider the hypothetical case of Mr. and Mrs. Johnson. After looking around, they have decided that they are interested in obtaining a brand-new Mercury Sable LS. The list price of the automobile is $18,982. They have found that they can purchase the car for $17,000 (the capital cost of the car).

If the Johnsons put 20 percent down and buy the car, the

salesman can get them a loan for 48 months at 10.9 percent. Assuming that the sales tax is $1,020 (6 percent) and license plates are $75, the total price is $18,095:

Capital Cost	$17,000
Sales Tax	1,020
License Plates	75
Total Price	$18,095

The down payment is therefore $3,619 (20 percent of $18,095). Their monthly payment is $372.10.

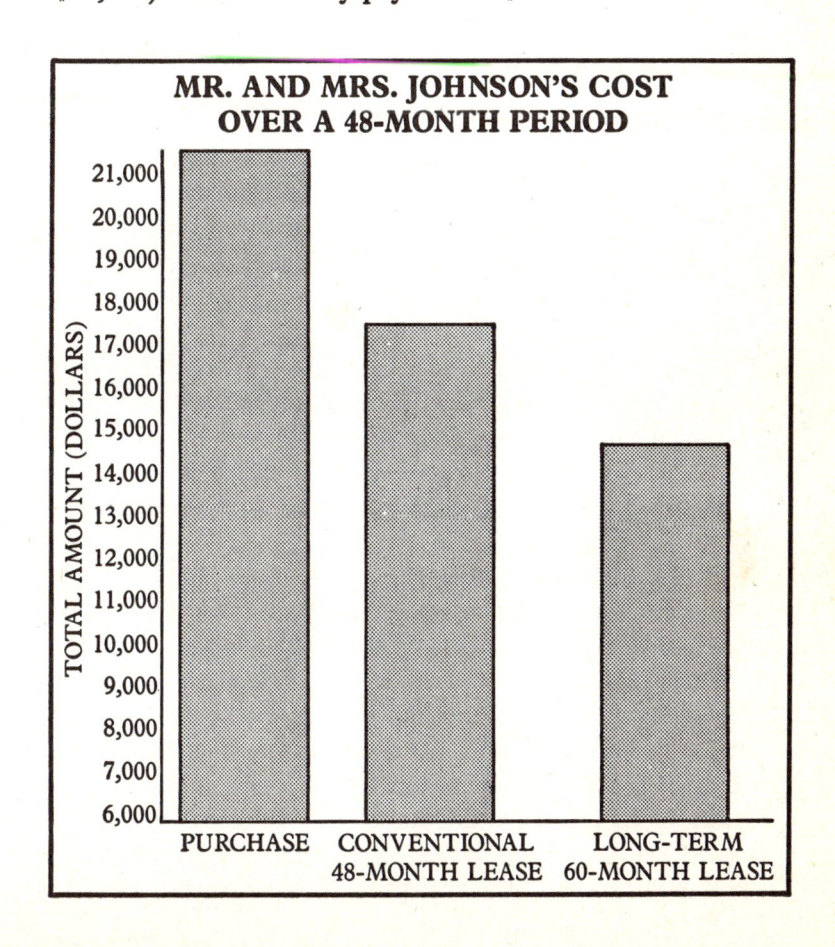

MR. AND MRS. JOHNSON'S COST OVER A 48-MONTH PERIOD

[Bar chart showing TOTAL AMOUNT (DOLLARS):
- PURCHASE: ~$21,400
- CONVENTIONAL 48-MONTH LEASE: ~$17,500
- LONG-TERM 60-MONTH LEASE: ~$14,600]

After 48 months, the Johnsons own their car outright. The only problem is that the Johnsons do not want to own their car anymore. They want to sell it and get a new one. They have forgone the interest they would have earned on their $3,619 down payment, and they cannot write off the interest that they paid to the bank or the sales tax that they paid to the state. They have spent $17,860.80 for their car payments over the four years, including the tax, for a grand total of $21,479.80:

Down payment	$ 3,619.00
Monthly payments	17,860.80
Total to purchase	$21,479.80

If the Johnsons decide instead to *lease* their new Mercury, they would not have to produce a costly down payment. They initially pay only the first payment and a security deposit (approximately one month's payment), as well as the registration, at the outset of the lease. Note that they do not have a big tax bill from the state either. Tax on a lease is paid on a monthly basis, and if the car is sold to a third party during or at the end of a lease, the tax remaining on the principal is paid by the new owner when he or she registers the purchase. This means that the new owner is paying no more and no less tax than he or she normally would on the used-car purchase, but the original lessee would pay tax only on the portion of the car that they actually used.

Also, if the Johnsons decide to lease, their down payment money can be put to other uses. Ten percent interest on $3,619 over four years would yield $1,679.58.

To illustrate the benefits of a long-term lease over a conventional lease term of three to four years, let us go back to the Johnsons. If the Johnsons use a conventional lease, they will spend $15,162.84 for a three-year lease (a monthly payment of $421.19 for 36 months) or $17,506.08 for a four-year lease ($364.71 per month for 48 months). Unfortunately, at the end of the lease, the car goes back to the bank at a bargain price. The 36-month residual is $7,023, but the car's estimated retail value is $10,750, nearly $3,750 higher. This is unfortunate both because the bank is taking advantage of the car's higher market value instead of the Johnsons (unless the Johnsons buy and then sell the car), and because a market value higher than the residual at the end of the lease means that the Johnsons paid a higher principal than they would have had to if the residual had been set higher. Similarly, at the end of 48 months, the bank owns this Mercury for the 48-month residual, $5,695, but the estimated wholesale value would be $8,500.

These estimates are based upon the NADA used-car guides, which give prices as a percentage of a car's list price. The National Auto Dealers Association (NADA) guides are the official used-car guides used by many dealers and lease banks for current retail, wholesale (trade-in), and loan values (the maximum amount a bank will loan for a particular car). There are other used-car guides, but NADA is most often quoted as a source, and I'll refer to that one for consistency. You can find a copy in your library or give your bank or insurance rep a call.

Finally, the Johnsons could choose a long-term lease. A low-residual, level-yield lease over 60 months will cost them $307.73 plus tax of $18.46 (at 6 percent) per month. They could choose to end the lease at 60 months, 48 months, 36 months, or at any time in between without losing money by buying out the lease and then selling the car. To buy out their lease, they would pay only the remaining principal plus the residual. The lease-end residual is set at $4,935.00 for this example, so the residual after 36 months would be $9,910.92, and it would be $7,422.96 for 48 months.

Because the Johnsons put average wear and tear on their car and it may not be a cream puff at the end of 36 months, the $9,910.92 they still owe the bank is closer to the value they would actually realize for the car than is the NADA retail price of $10,750 noted earlier. If they were to sell the car, then, by advertising in the newspaper after 36 months, using the retail market, they could safely expect to realize $9,900. They have thus achieved "retail equity"—what they owe the bank roughly equals what the car could get in the resale market (for instance, if the Johnsons sold the car themselves instead of traded it in). In a long-term, ALG lease, retail equity is reached at the end of 36 months—at the end of this time a person could sell the car and get out of the lease early without incurring additional costs. In this case, the Johnsons have saved some real money. They have spent only $11,742.84:

Monthly payments (including tax)	$326.19
× Months	36
Total after 36 months	$11,742.84

If the Johnsons did not want to sell the car on their own, they would have "wholesale equity" at the end of 48 months.

Reaching "wholesale equity" when the remaining principal and residual owed the bank equals the amount the car could be sold for in the wholesale market (if it were traded in, for example, to be resold at a higher retail price) takes longer—again because the price fetched will naturally be lower than a retail price. Estimates of the wholesale value place the car at $8,500, but once again, assume that the car is not a cream puff. The residual value of $7,422.96 is much closer to what the Johnsons will actually get by selling the car to a dealer; thus, they have wholesale equity. In this latter case, the Johnsons have used the car for a year longer and have spent a total of $15,657.12. They have also avoided the trouble of selling the car on their own. Just imagine the savings if they did sell it on their own at the end of 48 months!

The dollar figures over time are well worth comparing. The Johnsons can choose between paying $15,162.84 (with standard lease payments on a 36-month lease) or $11,742.84 (for 36 months of a 60-month level-yield, low-residual lease).

The difference is $3,420 in favor of the long-term lease. It's almost a certain bet that their car will not be worth $3,400 less than retail; thus they can make enough by selling the car to cover the cost of ending the lease.

LONG-TERM LEASES

- A long-term lease involves level payments of interest and principal over 60 months.
- This lease also incorporates a low residual value.
- Avoid leases in which the lender expects payment of unearned interest.
- If the lease is done correctly, the savings are large.
- This lease strategy makes better use of the market value of the leased car 36 to 48 months from the date of inception; since you pay a lower interest rate on a long-term lease, you pay more principal per month and thus achieve equity sooner—which means that you can sell the car for the actual market value after 36 or 48 months instead of allowing the bank to take advantage of a market value higher than the residual it received for the car.

SHORT-TERM LEASES

Although a long-term lease is financially advantageous, you should be looking for a short-term lease if you neither want to drive the same car for more than three years nor relish the thought of selling a car on your own three years hence (as you might do again if you signed a long-term lease to buy out early). A short-term auto lease is generally considered to be one that runs for 24 or 36 months.

In selecting a short-term lease, you'll want to weigh several criteria. The shorter the lease term, the less concerned you should be about the early termination costs. That is because people are unlikely to want to terminate a 24- or 36-month lease early. You should be sure that the lease is closed-end and that you will be able to walk away from the lease after the term is up. After that, your shopping should be concentrated on finding the lowest monthly payment.

Several programs on the market today are specifically designed for short-term leasing. One component of such a lease is an up-front down payment, sometimes called a *capital cost depreciator* or *capital cost reducer*. Making such a payment up front amounts to investing in someone else's depreciating asset—not a very appealing concept for the lessee. Mathematically it is difficult to justify. If the car were destroyed or stolen, you might find yourself with nothing to show for your investment. As a general rule, it is wise to avoid putting money down on a lease.

If you have purchased gap insurance (see Chapter 5), or had it included in the payment, your down payment becomes a further liability. Gap insurance will only pay the shortfall to the lease bank, not to you. Your down payment reduces that gap, thus reducing the value of the gap insurance, while increasing your vulnerability.

SHORT-TERM LEASES

- Short-term leases are only for those who are not comfortable with a lease for a longer term.
- The buyout option is not very important in the negotiation.
- The lease must be closed-end.
- The most important shopping criterion is the lowest monthly payment you can find.
- Avoid putting money down.

MANUFACTURER'S LEASES

At the time of this writing, several manufacturers, in concert with a lease bank (that is, the lease source that offers the financing), are offering some terrific lease deals on their cars. These manufacturers, all European at the moment, include BMW, Mercedes, Peugeot, and Volvo. The leases usually require no down payment (capital cost reducer or depreciator), and they run for a variety of terms. In all cases, the payment is substantially less than you would expect to pay with any other lease program. The active ingredient in these leases is a commitment from the manufacturer to the lease bank to pay for the difference between the wholesale value of the car at lease-end and the residual value.

So far, this book has described the residual value as an estimate of the auction value for the car at the time it comes off of the lease; however, in a manufacturer's lease, the residual value is purposely much greater. This is called over-residualization. The European manufacturers have found that artificially supporting the residual value has enormous benefits to their status-conscious marketing scheme by making the resale value of the automobile appear to be greater. The manufacturer is betting on a self-fulfilling prophecy to help increase the resale price at lease-end. In addition, the manufacturer is aware that certain customers will buy the car at lease-end for its high residual value. Others will have their car stolen or destroyed in an accident. Still others will decide that they want a new car early and buy out of the lease. In all of these cases, the customer pays the bank in full, and the manufacturer owes nothing.

Terminating a manufacturer's lease early, then, is very expensive. Therefore, to properly use the manufacturer's lease, you must be committed to keeping the car for the term of your lease. Otherwise, you will pay too much for the buyout, and you will be one of the people who make it inexpensive for everyone else.

What you should be looking for is an over-residualization about 20 percent higher than the anticipated auction value, which you'll be able to figure with the NADA trade-in figures. Take the longest term you are sure you will complete. The manufacturers know that the shorter a lease term, the greater the chances of completion, so the difference between actual auction value and residual value decreases with the term. Keep the car properly maintained and garaged. At lease-end, return the car to the selling dealer and walk away. This is the least expensive way to operate one of these cars for that term.

Currently no domestic manufacturers offer a good manufacturer's lease. Even though Ford Motor Credit, GMAC, and Chrysler Credit all have leasing branches, this does not necessarily mean that they have the type of program discussed here.

A manufacturer's lease can be the hardest kind to be approved for; the bank's criteria are among the most stringent in the market. You will be expected to be financially sound and without blemishes on your credit history. Lease banks will not be willing to help those who have not already established excellent credit.

Keep your leased car in excellent condition. The lease company will be very picky when you terminate the lease. If you are careful, a manufacturer's lease could be an excellent alternative to pursue.

MANUFACTURER'S LEASES

- Manufacturer's leases are not available on all makes and models.
- Manufacturer's leases set the residual value higher than the actual market value.
- The manufacturer's lease is a very expensive lease to terminate early.
- Take the longest term you know you will complete.
- Aim to return the car at lease-end, instead of buying it.
- This type of lease requires an excellent credit background.
- Use a manufacturer's lease only if you feel certain that you will keep the car neat and damage-free.

3
Special Strategies

Some drivers have special needs that require special strategies. For example, if you drive more than 15,000 miles a year, you may want to use a high-mileage leasing strategy. If you want to own your car, you may want to investigate leasing to buy. And if you use your car for business purposes, you should look into the tax strategies at the end of this chapter.

HIGH-MILEAGE STRATEGY

In general, auto leasing is most advantageous for those who drive fewer than 15,000 miles a year. But even if you drive a lot, you might want to lease a car to obtain benefits such as a luxury car for a less-than-luxury monthly payment. Strategies that would make leasing work would include the following ingredients:

- A short-term lease—it should not exceed 36 months.
- A high residual—You will not look to purchase this car or to buy out of the lease early. Therefore, the highest residual is most beneficial. In general, the highest residual is calculated in leases with a fair market value purchase option (that is, a purchase option stated not as a set amount at lease inception but as a formula, such as "the NADA wholesale figure at the end of the lease plus 5 percent") or in certain manufacturer's leases.
- Mileage in excess of 25,000 miles per year.

Most leases have an allowed mileage of 15,000 miles per year. Above 15,000 miles per year, there is a fixed mileage charge, usually 8 to 10 cents per mile. For this strategy to work, you should take out the lease with only the standard 15,000 miles per year.

Do *not* pay for the anticipated mileage before the lease-end. Most leases charge the same amount whether you pay for extra mileage at the beginning of the lease or at the end, so you save nothing by agreeing to make it part of your monthly payment. If you pay later, you can pay with dollars that have lost value to inflation, and you can invest the amount that you save on your monthly payments. Furthermore, if your car is stolen or destroyed during the lease term, you can get nothing back for the mileage that you haven't used. Also, if your job or your driving patterns change, you cannot receive compensation for all the miles you will never use.

Instead, at the end of the lease term, pay only for the miles that you actually have used. This amount could be less than anticipated.

Each mile above 15,000 is not worth exactly 8 cents, even if that is what you are charged. As the mileage grows, each mile becomes more valuable until each mile put on the car is worth more than 8 cents—that is, the car loses value at more than $.08 per mile at high mileages. At that time, the high-mileage strategy starts to pay off.

You benefit from the high-mileage strategy if the auction value of the car plus the excess-mileage fees total less than the residual value set in the lease. For example, imagine that the Johnsons sign a lease that sets a residual value of $7,500 after 36 months. This means that the bank will own that car after three years for $7,500. But remember, this is not necessarily the value of the car. If the car has 90,000 miles on the odometer (45,000 miles over the allowable 15,000 miles per year), the auction value of the car would be as low as $3,000. The bank would take a loss of $4,500 selling the car at auction. This plight is only partially mitigated by the excess-mileage penalty, which totals $3,600 (that is, $.08 × 45,000).

If the bank applies the penalty against the loss, it would still be short $900. In other words, the bank would own this car for $900 too much.

This strategy works better with more expensive cars, because they depreciate faster with excess mileage. The 36-month residual for a Lincoln Town Car with a list price of $31,000 would be $12,400. With 90,000 miles on the odometer, it would have a value of about $5,500. The excess-mileage fee would still be $3,600, and the bank would own this car for $3,300 too much.

This strategy does have several pitfalls to avoid. Because you don't pay for the excess mileage up front, do not forget that you will have to pay for any excess miles at a later date. This requires some fiscal responsibility; an amount like $3,600 may be difficult to come up with all at once.

HIGH-MILEAGE STRATEGY

- High mileage is an amount substantially over 15,000 miles per year.
- To make a high-mileage strategy work, you need a *short term* and *high residual* as well as *mileage in excess of 25,000 miles per year*.
- Do not use this strategy if you anticipate early termination of the lease or eventual purchase of the car.
- Pay for excess mileage *after* the term.
- The high-mileage strategy works better with more expensive cars.
- Do not forget to put money aside for the eventual excess-mileage fee.
- Be sure you can afford the usually higher monthly payments of a short-term lease.
- Keep reconditioning expenses at a minimum by taking good care of the car.

Also, payments for 36-month leases run substantially higher than on leases for longer terms. Pursue this strategy only if it won't break your budget.

Finally, pay extra attention to the servicing and general appearance of the car. Do not forget that the lease company requires that the car be returned with no more than average wear and tear. If the car is returned with 90,000 miles on it and it *looks* as if it has 90,000 miles on it, the reconditioning charges may eat up most of what you saved over the time of the lease.

TAX STRATEGIES FOR BUSINESS USE

Under current tax laws, individuals may not take deductions for the cost of a lease used for personal purposes. However, deductions are available for cars leased for business use. So if you are self-employed, a registered corporation, an officer of a corporation, or an individual who leases a car for business use, read on. Leasing means big savings in taxes.

General tax rules for leased cars are as follows. A company or individual may deduct the full amount of the lease payment and other expenses for the car's business use as long as the vehicle is used 100 percent for business. If the car is also used for pleasure, the individual or business may deduct only the portion of the leased car that is used for business (as long as the individual is not being reimbursed by his or her company). For example, if the cost of operating a vehicle for one year is $7,000 and 70 percent of that cost is attributable to business use, the total deduction is 70 percent of $7,000, or $4,900.

Many businesses find it more advantageous to take a 100 percent deduction for the lease and then issue a form 1099 to the driver, thereby reporting the personal portion of the lease as miscellaneous income paid to the driver. In the preceding example, the business would write off all $7,000 of the lease costs but would treat the $2,100 attributable to personal use as income of the driver, issuing a Form 1099 for that amount.

For luxury cars (any passenger vehicle with a capital cost greater than $12,800), the IRS has added a complex formula, designed to reduce the substantial advantage of leasing for tax deductions. This formula determines an offsetting amount, a portion of the car's value that the taxpayer must add to his or her gross income. To write off the lease expense, you will have to add this "inclusion amount" on your tax return.

Rather than expecting taxpayers to use the complex formula to calculate the inclusion amount, the IRS has published a table, reprinted here. To use the table, find the appropriate fair market value of your car in the left-hand column. In general, this amount is the manufacturer's suggested retail price (MSRP) or the total capitalized cost if it is included in the lease paperwork. At that row of the table, read across to find the column that corresponds to the year of the lease. The amount where this row and column intersect is the inclusion amount for the car in that tax year.

INCLUSION AMOUNTS FOR CARS FIRST LEASED IN 1989*

Fair Market Value Over	Not Over	1st	2nd	3rd	4th	5th & Later
$12,800	$13,100	$ 0	$ 0	$ 0	$ 1	$ 2
13,100	13,400	0	2	3	5	9
13,400	13,700	3	11	15	21	26
13,700	14,000	8	19	29	37	45
14,000	14,300	12	29	42	53	64
14,300	14,600	16	38	55	70	83
14,600	14,900	20	47	69	86	101
14,900	15,200	24	56	83	102	120
15,200	15,500	28	65	97	118	139
15,500	15,800	33	74	110	134	158
15,800	16,100	37	83	123	151	176
16,100	16,400	41	93	136	167	195
16,400	16,700	45	102	150	183	213
16,700	17,000	49	111	164	199	232
17,000	17,500	55	123	182	220	258
17,500	18,000	62	138	204	248	289
18,000	18,500	69	153	227	275	319
18,500	19,000	76	168	250	301	351
19,000	19,500	83	184	271	329	382

Year of Lease**

Special Strategies

Fair Market Value Over	Not Over	1st	2nd	Year of Lease** 3rd	4th	5th & Later
19,500	20,000	90	199	294	356	413
20,000	20,500	97	214	317	382	445
20,500	21,000	104	229	339	410	476
21,000	21,500	111	244	362	437	507
21,500	22,000	117	260	384	464	538
22,000	23,000	128	282	419	504	585
23,000	24,000	142	313	463	558	647
24,000	25,000	156	343	508	613	709
25,000	26,000	170	373	554	666	772
26,000	27,000	183	404	599	720	834
27,000	28,000	197	435	643	774	897
28,000	29,000	211	465	688	829	959
29,000	30,000	225	495	734	882	1,021
30,000	31,000	239	526	778	936	1,084
31,000	32,000	253	556	824	990	1,146
32,000	33,000	267	586	869	1,044	1,209
33,000	34,000	281	617	913	1,099	1,270
34,000	35,000	295	647	959	1,152	1,333
35,000	36,000	309	677	1,004	1,206	1,396
36,000	37,000	322	708	1,049	1,260	1,458
37,000	38,000	336	738	1,094	1,315	1,520
38,000	39,000	350	769	1,139	1,368	1,583
39,000	40,000	364	799	1,184	1,423	1,664
40,000	41,000	378	829	1,230	1,476	1,707
41,000	42,000	392	860	1,274	1,530	1,770
42,000	43,000	406	890	1,319	1,585	1,832
43,000	44,000	420	920	1,365	1,638	1,894
44,000	45,000	434	951	1,409	1,693	1,956
45,000	46,000	448	981	1,454	1,747	2,019
46,000	47,000	461	1,012	1,499	1,801	2,081
47,000	48,000	475	1,042	1,545	1,854	2,144
48,000	49,000	489	1,073	1,589	1,909	2,205
49,000	50,000	503	1,103	1,634	1,963	2,268
50,000	51,000	517	1,133	1,680	2,016	2,331
51,000	52,000	531	1,164	1,724	2,071	2,393
52,000	53,000	545	1,194	1,770	2,124	2,455
53,000	54,000	559	1,224	1,815	2,179	2,517
54,000	55,000	573	1,255	1,859	2,233	2,580
55,000	56,000	587	1,285	1,905	2,286	2,643
56,000	57,000	600	1,316	1,950	2,340	2,705
57,000	58,000	614	1,346	1,995	2,395	2,767
58,000	59,000	628	1,376	2,041	2,448	2,829
59,000	60,000	642	1,407	2,085	2,502	2,892

*These figures are for approximation only. Since depreciation and inflation change, the IRS issues a revised table at the end of each year. Obtain the most up-to-date revision to assure an accurate inclusion amount.

**For the last tax year of the lease, use the dollar amount for the preceding year.

For example, assume that Mr. Jones leased a car on January 1. The MSRP on the car was $26,775. The car was leased for the business only and will be used 100 percent for business. At the end of the year, the inclusion amount would be figured by finding the row in the table that corresponds to a fair market value of $26,775. This is the row for values over $26,000 but not over $27,000. Reading across the table to the column for the first year of the lease, the inclusion amount is $183. Therefore, Mr. Jones will add $183 to his gross income, offsetting some of the benefit of the deduction for the cost of the lease.

If the business use of the car is less than 100 percent, the offsetting income, like the lease expense, should be reduced to reflect only the proportion of the car used for business. For example, if during the second year of his lease, Mr. Jones decides that he will use the car for personal travel 30 percent of the time, he will have to adjust the inclusion amount accordingly. First, he looks across the table for the second year's inclusion amount, which is $404. Next he finds the percentage of this amount that is attributable to business use (the 70 percent of the use not attributable to personal travel):

$$\$404 \times 70\% = \$283$$

Finally, if the lease is started or terminated on any day other than January 1, the offsetting income must be reduced by the number of days that the car was not in service. For example, assume that Mr. Jones terminates the lease on July 15 in the third year of the contract. Until that time, he was still using the car 70 percent for business. First he finds the third-year amount in the table: $599. This amount is multiplied by the portion of business use *and* by the portion of the year the car was in service:

$$\$599 \times 70\% \times 53.4\% \ (195/365) = \$224$$

Notice that the portion of the year the car was in service is simply the number of days in service divided by the total number of days in a year (365).

Since a company auto insurance policy is often significantly more expensive than personal insurance, an important money-saving strategy would be to lease and insure the car in the name of a corporate officer directly. At the same time, the

TAX STRATEGIES FOR BUSINESS USE

- Leasing for tax deductions will help the self-employed person, business, or individual using the car for business.
- Tax deductions for leasing are many times realized more quickly than for purchasing, as the cost of a lease is spread over two to five years (depending on the term), instead of the *required* 5 years for purchased vehicles.
- The basic tax deduction on an auto lease is for the cost of the lease times the percentage of business use.
- Any personal use of a business lease must not be deducted, or else must be treated as miscellaneous income to the driver (which the employer reports on Form 1099).
- Business deductions for auto leases must be partially offset by an IRS-specified inclusion amount.
- To reduce the cost of auto insurance, a business lease may be taken out in the name of an individual.
- This strategy provides little benefit when used for cars with a capital cost of less than $16,000, since below that the cost of a purchased car for business use is tax deductible. Above that, the cost of a purchased car cannot be deducted whereas the cost of a leased car can be.

company should pay all costs of leasing and upkeep of the car. Because the company pays these amounts as a perk to the officer, they are deductible under the rules just stated, yet the insurance rate is about half of what it would have been if the company leased the car in its own name.

Making the officer the lessee works only if the officer is willing to assume a financial risk for the benefit of the company. Therefore, this option is usually reserved for the owners of companies.

A business lease has its limits. It does little for cars with a capital cost of less than $16,000, because a business can take the same amount of deductions in only five years by depreciating a purchased car of that value. The company would also have equity in the purchased car.

LEASING TO BUY

Leasing a car and purchasing it for the cost of the residual at lease-end often makes sense. Many times it's cheaper than purchasing through traditional financing, and even if you don't want to keep the car at lease-end you can sell it and many times come out ahead, as long as the car has been kept in good shape.

A closed-end lease should mean that you are not putting money down to start the lease (called a "front-end balloon"). It should also mean that you are getting the option to purchase the car at lease-end (called a "back-end balloon"). As you shift the balloon from the front end to the back end of a contract, this cost becomes less expensive in terms of constant dollars.

For example, if inflation averages 5 percent per year, compounded over five years, each dollar spent at the end of the term would be worth only 74 cents in today's dollars. Therefore, a $5,000 purchase option five years from now would have the same purchasing power as $3,700 today. If the residual is reasonably low and the payments are attractive, you would be better off to use a lease as alternative financing

Special Strategies

than to spend the same amount of money to buy a car the traditional way. In this chapter you'll find formulas to compare the costs of leasing to buy versus purchasing.

If you use this strategy, some leases must be avoided. Leasing to buy is not recommended for manufacturer's leases (see Chapter 2). Their residuals are artificially high and will exceed the actual value of the car at lease-end. The value of a manufacturer's lease is in returning the car at lease-end.

Also, this strategy is risky with leases that use fair-market-value residuals (as opposed to fixed purchase options, which set the buyout value of the car at lease inception instead of lease-end). When the residual is not set at the lease's inception, it becomes difficult to compare the monetary advantages of various contracts.

It is worthwhile to compare the total cost of a purchase with the total cost of leasing to purchase. To estimate the cost to purchase, you can use the following formula:

Down payment (including sales tax on entire purchase price)   *1,000*
+ Monthly payment × term   *300 × 36*   *10,800*
+ Unearned interest on down payment, adjusted for inflation (what this money could have earned if invested instead of used to buy a car)   *1000 × .025*   *25.00*
_____
= Total cost of purchasing

The total cost of leasing to purchase can be estimated with the following formula:

Monthly payment × term (including sales tax)*
+ Residual (assuming a fixed purchase option)
+ Tax on residual
− Adjustment for the effects of inflation on the constant-dollar value of the residual
_____
= Total cost of leasing to purchase

_____
*Usually the monthly cost of the lease × the applicable sales tax rate, but it varies from state to state.

With regard to this second formula, remember that the residual amount is set at the beginning of the lease term, but you don't pay it until lease-end. Therefore, you need to adjust for the amount by which inflation erodes the real value of the residual payment. To figure that correct amount in your own calculations, use the constant dollar adjustment chart by multiplying every hundred dollars of your residual by the amount corresponding to an estimate of the inflation rate and the correct number of years. This is what your residual will be worth in future dollars at the end of your lease. The difference between the current and future amounts is the amount to subtract when taking the effects of inflation on your residual into account.

CONSTANT DOLLAR ADJUSTMENT CHART: THE VALUE OF $100 IN FUTURE YEARS

	Inflation Rate	Year 1	Year 2	Year 3	Year 4	Year 5
$100	3.0%	$97.00	$94.09	$91.27	$88.53	$84.87
100	4.0	96.00	92.16	88.47	84.94	81.54
100	5.0	95.00	90.25	85.74	81.45	77.38
100	6.0	94.00	88.36	83.06	78.08	73.39
100	7.0	93.00	86.49	80.44	74.81	69.57
100	8.0	92.00	84.64	77.87	71.64	65.91
100	9.0	91.00	82.81	75.36	68.58	62.40
100	10.0	90.00	81.00	72.90	65.61	59.05

To see how to use these formulas, imagine that the Johnsons are trying to decide between buying or leasing to purchase a $17,000 Mercury Sable. Assume that if they buy the car, they will make a down payment of $3,606 and borrow $14,424 at 10.9 percent for 60 months. Instead of using the $3,606 to buy the car, they could have invested it at 10 percent compounded annually. Their total costs of purchasing would be as follows:

Down payment	$ 3,606.00
Monthly payments	18,773.00
Unearned interest (adjusted for inflation)	1,707.45
Total to purchase	$24,086.45

Instead, the Johnsons could sign a lease specifying a residual value of $4,935.00 after five years and total monthly payments of $19,571.40. At 6 percent, the tax on the residual you pay when purchasing the car at lease-end would be $296.10. Assuming 5 percent inflation for five years, the residual would lose $1,307.78 of its value in constant dollars. The total price of leasing to purchase would therefore be as follows:

Monthly payments	$19,571.40
Residual	4,935.00
Tax on residual	296.10
Less: Adjustment for inflation on the residual	(1,307.78)
Total to lease to purchase	$23,494.72

Finding the difference between these two totals shows that purchasing the Sable through a lease would save the Johnsons $591.73 in terms of constant dollars. In fact, it can save much more. For the sake of simplicity, the example sets the lease interest rate at 10.9 percent to compete with the loan rate; however, lease rates are generally lower than loan rates. If the lease rate were merely a percentage point lower, the saving would be over $1,100.

Be sure to do the math! Not all lessors are the same. Some bump the price of the purchase option up on the contract so it is higher than the residual value set in the lease. In the event of a purchase or early termination, this higher figure is used to compute the costs to the lessee, and the additional amount over and above the residual is sheer additional profit to the dealer. To avoid this scam, simply check the total price by using these formulas. A lease price a great deal larger than the purchase price may indicate that the price of the purchase option has been bumped up on your lease.

LEASING TO BUY

- With a leasing-to-buy strategy, you move the largest single payment from the beginning of a contract (as with a down payment) to the end of a contract, thereby using inflation to help you minimize your costs.
- If the payments and residual are low enough that your costs for leasing to buy are less than those for purchasing, then leasing becomes the least expensive form of financing.
- Do not mix the leasing-to-buy strategy with manufacturer's leases or leases with fair-market-value purchase options.
- Before electing this strategy for any particular car, compare the total cost of leasing to buy with the total cost of purchasing.
- Make sure that the math works! Your lease purchase option amount may have been "bumped" up from the residual figure, a scam that only means additional dealer profit.

4
Shopping for a Lease

To get the best deal on a lease, you need to be an informed shopper. Before you head for an auto dealership, arm yourself by reviewing the information in this chapter. You'll learn how the dealership figures the cost of a lease, how to identify the best deal, sneaky sales tactics to beware of, and what terms you can expect in a lease contract.

FIGURING THE COST OF A LEASE

When the lease manager goes to the computer or starts to figure on a worksheet, he or she invokes a multitude of formulas to figure the monthly payment. To understand these formulas, you must understand what the lease manager is doing so you can trust the figures he or she comes up with.

First he or she establishes the property being leased. As an example, let us use the hypothetical car that the Johnsons ended up leasing. This car is a new Mercury Sable LS. The list price of the car (MSRP) is $18,982. The car was capitalized (selling price) for $17,000. The lease manager must determine the residual value of the car. Remember that this is what the bank figures to be the fail-safe value of the car at the end of the lease term—in other words, the high bid they could expect to receive when they send the car to auction. The bank is in the money business and not in the car business, so it is not interested in stretching the residual value too far. Depending on the type of car and its market value, a residual of 25–45 percent of the original price is typical on a four-year lease. (The ALG residual guide is updated regularly to show what the leasing industry predicts the value of cars will be after various numbers of years. Checking it will help you determine your car's approximate residual for comparing leasing to buying.) In this case, the residual is 25 percent of the MSRP after 60 months, or $4,745.50.

Then the interest rate must be figured. This is often converted to a money factor rate, which is the average percentage of interest paid on the principal each month. A yield percentage (interest rate) of 10 percent would translate into a money factor of .004165, for example. The accompanying chart shows a range of interest rates and corresponding money factors:

Interest Rate	Money Factor	Interest Rate	Money Factor
9.00%	.003743	11.00%	.004589
9.25%	.003849	11.25%	.004695
9.50%	.003954	11.50%	.004801
9.75%	.00406	11.75%	.004907
10.00%	.004165	12.00%	.005014
10.25%	.004271	12.25%	.00512
10.50%	.004377	12.50%	.005226
10.75%	.004483	12.75%	.005333

These money factors may not be the exact amounts used by the lease manager. He or she may use a rounded-off number, as yields will vary slightly depending upon the term. However, these factors will certainly be close enough to illustrate the origin of the lease payment figure the lease manager comes up with.

Assuming that the Johnsons' lease manager offers an interest rate of 10 percent, the facts of the transaction can be summarized as follows:

Term:	60 months
MSRP:	$18,982.00
Capital Cost:	$17,000.00
Residual Value:	$4,745.50
Interest Rate:	10% (.0042 money factor rate)

In addition to the capital cost of the car, most banks require a sign-up fee. This is a fixed amount of money, added to the capital cost of the car, that offsets the expense of setting up the account and processing the paperwork. In this example, the set-up cost will be $300. So in addition to the previous information, we must add:

Bank Fee: $300.00

Since the lease payments cover the depreciation of the car over the period of the term, the first calculation is to add the bank fee to the capital cost and then to subtract the residual to find the total depreciation you will be paying on the car over the lease term:

Bank Fee	$ 300.00
Capital Cost	17,000.00
Less: Residual	(4,745.50)
Depreciation	$12,554.50

Then divide the total depreciation amount by the months in the term. This figure becomes the average monthly depreciation:

$$\$12,554.50 \div 60 \text{ months} = \$209.24/\text{month}$$

To figure the interest, the lease manager will apply the yield percentage to the amount the Johnsons borrow—the capital cost of the car. However, it is important to remember that the residual value of the leased vehicle is an *undepreciating capital cost*. In other words, no part of the monthly payment ever offsets that residual. To make up for the fact that the yield is based on declining capital costs (the principal), the average yield per month must be based instead on capital cost plus the bank fee plus the residual value (the bank expects interest on the end-value of the car they are loaning you, i.e., the residual). To compute the average interest on the declining amount and the nondeclining residual value at the same time, begin by totaling the sum of:

Bank Fee	$ 300.00
Capital Cost	17,000.00
Residual	4,745.50
Total	$22,045.50

The money factor is then applied to this total to compute the monthly interest:

$$\$22{,}045.50 \times .0042 = \$92.59$$

Now simply add the monthly depreciation to the monthly interest charges to find the total monthly payment:

Monthly Depreciation	$209.24
Monthly Interest	92.59
Monthly Payment	$301.83

To this figure, you may have to add sales tax. In most states, the tax is simply calculated as the monthly cost of the lease times the applicable sales tax rate in your area. For example, if the sales or use tax is 6 percent, then the total payment would look like this:

Monthly Payment	$301.83
Tax (at 6%)	18.11
Total Monthly Payment	$319.94

In some states, including New Jersey, the sales tax is added to the capital cost of the car. The tax then becomes a part of the payment. As an example, in New Jersey the most common method of figuring sales tax is to take 6 percent of the sum of the bank fee and the capital cost minus the residual:

Bank Fee	$ 300.00
Capital Cost	17,000.00
Less: Residual	(4,745.50)
Total Taxable Amount	$12,554.50

$$\text{Tax } 6\% \times \$12{,}554.50 = \$753.27$$

With this method, the tax is then included in the amount to be depreciated:

Bank Fee	$ 300.00
Capital Cost	17,000.00
Tax	753.27
Less: Residual	(4,745.50)
Depreciation	$13,307.77

As before, divide the total depreciation by the number of months to find the average monthly depreciation:

$13,307.77 ÷ 60 months = $221.80/month

Likewise, the tax is included in the calculation of monthly interest:

Bank Fee	$ 300.00
Capital Cost	17,000.00
Tax	753.27
Residual	4,745.50
Total	$22,798.77

$22,798.77 × .0042 = $95.75

Also as before, the total monthly payment equals the monthly depreciation plus the monthly interest:

Monthly Depreciation	$221.80
Monthly Interest	95.75
Total Monthly Payment	$317.55

As the same tax rates are assumed, it might seem confusing that the monthly payment in New Jersey is lower than the previous figure. But further examination will reveal that the New Jersey amount is based on the total depreciation of the car over the lease term, whereas most taxes are based upon total depreciation *plus* interest charged.

Other taxes need to be paid in various states. For example, some states assess a property tax on the leased property.

However, these taxes are carefully stated outside the lease payment and should not cause confusion.

To parallel the work being done by the lease manager, you will need to ask certain questions:

- What is the capital cost (that is, the selling price)?
- What is the bank fee, if any?
- What is the residual value?
- If the residual is given as a percentage of the list price, then what is the list price? (Some domestic manufacturers have discounts for certain packages that are built into the automobile. These discounts mean that there are, in effect, two list prices. To calculate the residual, always use the higher price.)
- What percentage rate is the effective yield?

If the information is factual and you have correctly done the math, your figures should not vary widely from those of the lease manager.

SMILIN' SAMMY IN THE LEASE OFFICE

"There's a sucker born every minute" is the famous quote of P. T. Barnum. Some say that he was the greatest showman of the twentieth century, and while that may be argued, he clearly was one of the most perceptive.

With the same kind of flair and showmanship, thousands of merchants, with hundreds of thousands of employees, twist claims and the English language in order to deliberately perpetuate fraud among the general population. Leasing has its share of these Smilin' Sammys. Of course, while underhanded tactics such as those described here are used from time to time, not all or even most dealerships will use them.

Don't be afraid to look for a car lease, but do bring a healthy amount of skepticism with you to the lease office. A deal that sounds too good to be true is probably just that.

The savings that result from using the various strategies

described in this book, like any other good reward, come from understanding what is going on and from doing some hard work. It stretches the imagination to think that someone could be offering deals that save many thousands of dollars. To avoid mistakes, you need a good understanding of what the dealership is really offering.

Deceptive Ads

For some typical examples, consider an ad that recently ran in the *Bergen Record*, a regional paper that serves northern New Jersey. The headline reads, "NO DOWN PAYMENT!!" Below that, subheadlines read, "36 Months at 60-Month Rates!" and, "Your Option, Terminate or Purchase After First Year."

Following these headlines is a list of "sale prices" for a great variety of cars—for example, a Lincoln Mark VII for $319 per month. A little arithmetic shows that over three years, this $28,000 car would cost only $11,484 to operate. That includes interest on $28,000 for three years.

Finally, some small print appears near the bottom of the ad:

> These are lease transactions. 1st pymt. & sec. dep. due at inception. Dealer prep. incl. Lessee resp. for wear & tear. Cars factory std. equip. For total pymt., multiply by 60. 20% CR on Porsche, MB, BMW & Lincoln.

This short, inconspicuous paragraph is a work of art. In its jumble of hard-to-read abbreviations, it nullifies everything that was screamed out in the clearer print. The advertised prices were not for 36-month leases. If we must multiply the payment by 60 for the total price, these must be 60-month leases. These are not no-down-payment leases. The expression "20% CR" stands for 20 percent cash reduction. A cash reduction is a euphemism for a down payment. Therefore, on a $28,000 car, there is a down payment of $5,600! Furthermore, "std. equip." indicates that none of the cars described include options. You would expect to pay quite a bit more for a car that is worth driving.

Most puzzling is the statement "Lessee resp. for wear & tear." In all leases, a lessee is responsible for *excess* wear and tear, but the only time a lessee is responsible for wear and tear is when he is responsible for the resale value of the car at lease-end. In other words, this is an open-end lease, and the lessee must pledge to make up any shortfall between the negotiated residual value and the actual value received at lease termination.

Finally, look at the headline "Your Option, Terminate or Purchase After First Year." Almost any lease can be voluntarily terminated after any amount of time. The unanswered questions are "At what price?" and "With what strings attached?" Often too late lessees find themselves on the wrong side of a lease that will cost them thousands of dollars to get out of.

So on second look, this lease company's leases do not seem so attractive.

It seems that Smilin' Sammy's ads are limited only by his imagination. In addition to the group of deceits described in this example, a popular way of transforming a small price into a larger one is the "introductory offer." In this scenario, a very low figure is prominently displayed in the most readable section of the ad. Below this is a general list of all the benefits that the price includes and the mandatory "no money down." What is not revealed until the small print is that the figures quoted in the ad are an "introductory price" good only for the first six months of the lease. At the end of the six months, the price of the leased vehicle will rise to a figure that is not disclosed in the ad and is frequently not disclosed at all until the time of delivery.

Other Tactics

Unfortunately, the automotive section of your daily paper is not the only place where Smilin' Sammy plies his deceptive trade. He has a plethora of scams in store for the unwary customer.

Bait-and-switch tactics are as common in the leasing business as elsewhere in retail sales. If the salesperson lures you into the lease office with a great deal only to talk you out of it once you get there, by all means stop the discussion long enough to be sure that he or she is still working for your better interests. If you have to go home to think about it, then go home. The atmosphere of a showroom is not always conducive to clear thinking. The salesperson may have lured you in on an open-end lease, only to tell you of its many hazards once you arrive in the office. When the salesperson gives you the price for "the better lease," you may not have enough information to determine whether that price is fair or not.

In another popular move, the lease person admits with a glum face that he or she was unable to locate (or get you approved for) the car for which you made a deal. However, on the brighter side, he or she was able to find (or get you approved for) a different car that is certain to have a different pricing schedule.

This last tactic is popular with the bait-and-switch artists. Average people will be lured to a Mark VII by the great price. When they find out that they "misread" the ad in the paper, they are assured that they have no real problem because the lease company can do a Thunderbird for the same price and no money down.

Another popular antic is the "lowball" tactic. A lessee is lured into the lease office by a great telephone quote, couched in terms of "around," "about," "more or less," or "If I could get you. . . ." When the lessee arrives, the price gets "bumped" up $50 or $60 a month. While that does not sound like a lot of money to the novice, it means $2,500 added gross profit to the dealer of the car on a 60-month lease.

At delivery time, the contract is not even available until the insurance is verified and the routine paperwork is completed. There the customers sit, surrounded by their children. They have told the neighbors that they are coming home with a new car today. Then the contract arrives. The car includes rustproofing and undercoating, which the lease manager explains is the only way the lease company could get the car from the dealership, and the monthly price is $50 higher still. Novice lessees may find that deal difficult to walk away from.

If they hesitate, they may find themselves in the office of another manager. That "manager" is in fact a closer, someone paid specifically to gather the last dollar of profit possible before the car goes out the door. This person is generally much better armed than the buyers for four reasons:

1. The closer is not in love with the car. He or she can remain dispassionate about the negotiating process, which is usually harder for the customers.
2. The closer understands the arcane leasing formulas and is always aware of where he stands financially in a deal. The customers rarely understand where the numbers for the lease payment are coming from and must rely somewhat upon the closer.
3. The closer has had tremendous experience finding what turns people on and will take advantage of these "hot buttons." In general, the customers are only novices at concealing their interests and interpreting those of the closer.
4. The customers have already made the mental commitment to lease.

The closer will work with the customers and justify the price increase in terms that he or she feels will satisfy them. If necessary, the closer will renegotiate the deal downward, but he or she will definitely take every dollar possible before the car is delivered.

In addition to "lowball," Smilin' Sammy also knows "highball." When Smilin' sees that a customer obviously wants to negotiate the best deal he can—that is, he wants to see a big difference between the first amount quoted him by the dealer and the final figure they agree upon—Smilin' hits the customer with the highest number he can imagine. The purpose is to come down in large increments, all the time making the customer feel that he is a stronger negotiator than Smilin'. Finally the customer feels that he has taken all that he could reasonably demand, while the dealer still comes away with a high profit margin.

Here is another way that Smilin' Sammy can be adept at turning your shopping practices against you. Many shoppers have learned the tactic of "springing the trade." While the value of such a tactic is certainly questionable, there are many who feel they can get a better price buying a car when they claim no trade-in until the price of the car is settled. At that time, they enter into a separate negotiation over the price of the trade. (This tactic is considered controversial because it tends to alienate the dealer and implies that you cannot negotiate in good faith.)

Smilin' Sammy will use this tactic to his advantage. He will "allow" a very high price for the trade-in and then "back out" the payment to take account of the trade—that is, reduce the monthly payment figure by working the formula backwards so that the capital cost of the car satisfies a given monthly payment instead of the other way around. In many cases, the customer is unable to see the actual value that was allowed for the car. Indeed, if Smilin' Sammy is adept enough, he can completely steal the trade. With all of the other figures the customer is trying to keep track of, the quote he or she got when holding back the trade could be the one that appears on the contract at the time of delivery. Someone at some time will neglect to spot the "oversight."

The average person, sans portable computer, will be hard put to keep up with the mathematical dexterity of the dishonest and determined lease agent. As a precaution, it is advisable to negotiate the deal without a trade-in and then to ask for a check in payment for the trade-in amount. If you were counting on the trade-in to lower the monthly payment to a figure that you could more easily afford, deposit the check in an interest-bearing account. Each month, deduct the amount you need from the account, and leave the rest to grow. By following this method, you will avoid being taken on your trade-in. In addition, the money you deposit will continue to perform for you while offsetting the higher payments. Finally, should your leased car meet an unfortunate end, you will be the one holding the dollars, not the lease dealer or the bank.

A variation on taking the trade-in money as a check and accepting the higher monthly payment is to use the check to pay off high-interest items such as the balance on your Visa or other credit cards. As these accounts often charge around 20 percent, you would more than save the difference between the lower lease payment and the higher lease payment that you finally accepted.

In any case, consider this: a business that is willing to play games in the showroom will play games with the security deposit, the payments, and every aspect of your transaction. Is that the lease company you want to do business with?

While many of the tactics described here are "only" unethical, they are often supported by practices that are actually illegal. A whole slew of consumer laws are on the books to protect against bait-and-switch advertisements or "asterisks" advertisements that relegate facts to the footnotes, yet these laws are broken every day.

It is important to recognize the villain in all of these various schemes. It is not only the floor salespeople, who go through their paces like well-trained monkeys. It is not only the managers, who cling desperately to their newly acquired veneer of respectability. The blame must rest squarely upon the shoulders of the ownership, for only at this level can the deceit be put to rest by edict, and only at this level can the deceit find the funds to propagate itself.

The lies will not stop as long as the people in charge believe that "a sucker is born every minute." No wonder, like P. T. Barnum, so many callous hawkers feel compelled to dress up their advertisements in carnival trappings.

SMILIN' SAMMY IN THE LEASE OFFICE

- Be wary of deals that sound too good to be true. They probably are.
- Read the small print. The awkward abbreviations and chopped sentences may take away everything that the big type promises.
- Beware of bait-and-switch tactics.
- Beware of the "lowball" or the "highball." These tactics are as common in the lease industry as elsewhere in sales.
- Beware of the "bump"—a price that is inflated at delivery time.
- Do not accept a renegotiated deal at delivery time.
- Try to make the trade-in a separate deal, and ask to have the trade-in amount paid by check.

FINDING THE BEST DEAL

Smilin' Sammy is not the easiest person to spot. He does not necessarily wear a plaid jacket with a loud tie anymore, and his voice might have the sonorous timbre of a radio announcer rather than resembling the loutish braying of an old-time vaudevillian.

This should come as no surprise. Would you leave your multimillion-dollar business in the hands of someone dressed like the court jester? Modern dealerships wouldn't either, so they recruit college-educated people who will present themselves as more like lawyers than flamboyant hustlers out to make you their next mark.

This means that a customer's approach to finding the best deal on a lease should depend upon more than superficial surroundings. You will have to judge each quote on its own merit. That means shopping.

Since few customers would be able to follow Smilin' Sammy's calculations while he is making them, use the following guidelines to assure you get a good deal.

Select a Strategy

First you should decide which strategy would be best for you. The Johnsons have decided that a long-term lease with an early termination is perfect for them. Therefore, when they shop for a lease, it does them no good to compare a 60-month manufacturer's lease with a 60-month lease designed for an early termination. It is highly unlikely that the Johnsons would be able to terminate a manufacturer's lease early without owing thousands of dollars. Since early termination is their desire, they must shop the same ALG leases from dealer to dealer. It is the basic lease guide and usually has the lowest recorded residual values. (See the discussion of long-term leases in Chapter 2.) For the Johnsons, it will be important to find a lease that uses both an ALG residual and a level-yield interest rate.

Shop Around

Once you are satisfied that a quote you have received is on the right type of contract, go to another dealership and check that quote against a similar car, using a similar strategy. If you are comparing dissimilar cars, you may need to use some rules of thumb.

If you have found two similar cars, with similar contracts, compare the numbers; remember that $10 per month on a 60-month lease means a difference of $500. If there is a gross discrepancy, you may wish to simply give your order to the better dealership or to contact the higher dealership with the lower offer. If the numbers are close, then your decision should be based on your preference in dealerships, proximity to home or work, color selection, and any intangibles that affect your relationship to your car.

Where the difference in price is not dramatic, the sale should go to the dealership that is going to support you better. A car is not a toaster oven or a can of peas. A car needs regular maintenance and an occasional repair. The vehicle's reliability is directly related to the support system designed to handle its upkeep when it goes back to the shop. A lease or purchase should therefore be viewed as something of a marriage, where the continued support of the car is as crucial as the final price of the car. If the dealership has a poor reputation, then price should not be a factor at all—a poor dealership cannot make you happy, no matter what price you are quoted.

If you are shopping two different cars, the job becomes much more subjective, and price comparisons become difficult. A Buick and a Mercury may have similar prices but substantially different lease rates. This could come about because of a promotion by the manufacturer, a difference in residual values, or a keener desire to make a deal by one or another of the dealers. In such a case, use these rules of thumb to decide which car is best for you:

- In a 60-month lease, every $2 of lease payment a month is worth about $100 of principal. This principal can be added dealer profit or difference in residual values.
- In a 48-month lease, every $2.50 a month is worth about $100 of principal.
- In a 36-month lease, every $3.40 a month is worth about $100 of principal.
- In a 24-month lease, every $4.75 a month is worth about $100 of principal.

In each of these cases, you must decide whether the car you want to drive for the next several years is worth the difference in principal. Using the same rules of thumb, you can find out how much more or less you are being charged from one store to another for the same model of automobile.

Also shop for the best terms for the up-front costs. When you start the lease, you will be asked to pay the first month's payment. You will also be asked to pay a security deposit that will be in the neighborhood of one month's payment. One month rounded up to the next $25 is common. Finally, you will be expected to pay any fees related to registration and up-front taxes that might be expected where you live.

There are some variations on this theme, but if the variance is large, it should be viewed with suspicion. If a lease company wants a security deposit equal to six months' payments, ask whether the security deposit will earn interest. In most cases it will not; then you have to calculate the interest lost against the payment quoted to make sure that you still have the best deal. Some lease companies will waive the security deposit altogether, and to compensate they will raise the interest rate they are charging. Is not paying the extra month's payment, which you should be getting back at lease termination anyway, worth paying the extra monthly fee?

Some lease companies tout special programs that feature a large down payment. The rates quoted are low, but the down payment and all the interest it could have earned are lost forever. Besides, one of the most appealing reasons for leasing is to stop investing in a depreciating asset.

Watch Out for Fatigue

Many dealerships are not interested in your need to shop the price from one dealership to another. They will try any strategy to "stop the shopper." In fact, there is hardly a sales seminar that does not cover this topic for all salespeople, lease people included.

The most jaded might conclude that the dealer has this desire to stop the shopper because he or she *knows* that the price is too high and fears that the customer might discover this on the very next stop. While there are undoubtedly dealers who have just that fear, the great majority of dealers fear a much more mundane human condition: fatigue. Remember that a $100 shift in dealer profit means only $2 a month in the payments on a 60-month lease. A shopper who has been on car lots since nine in the morning will not be willing to travel back to the first dealer visited unless there is a big payment difference between that dealer and the current one. Since the customer is armed with the early figures, he or she is much more willing to inform the current dealer of his or her "best price," to see whether the current dealer can match it and save another trip to the first dealer. It is true that a dealer would much rather be the last dealer that a customer visits than the most competitive.

This point is especially important if your judgment has been clouded by the combination of tiredness, offers, counteroffers, and the plethora of technical information that accompanies each visit to a dealership. If so, you are not properly equipped to make a decision. Go back the next day when you are refreshed.

"But what can we do to put you in this car today?" intones the lease manager. If you are not willing to put down a deposit on the spot, you might find out that the residual value will change the next day, or the special of the week will be over. In fact, your soul might be lost to the devil for all eternity if you do not make a commitment *now*! Or so the lease manager would have you believe.

In fact, residuals will change at the beginning of the month. If you are shopping on the last day of the month, the lease manager is probably telling the truth, at least with regard to the residual. Offer to fill out a credit application right away. If the bank approves the credit application before the residual changes, you will have a reasonable time to get the contract filled out and the car delivered. Do not leave a deposit. It's not necessary, and it's not smart when you are tired and confused. If you are sure that you have the right deal, you can always come back the following day and leave the deposit.

Finally, most communities have a Better Business Bureau. If you are unsure of the reputation of the dealership or lease business that you are dealing with, then call the Better Business Bureau. Be sure that the outfit that is going to take your money is the one you want to do business with.

FINDING THE BEST DEAL

- Decide which lease strategy you wish to pursue, then compare quotes that use only that strategy.
- Shop around for lease quotes, and judge each quote on its own merits.
- Judge the dealership. It may be worth the extra money to go with one over the other.
- If you are comparing two different cars, use the formulas given to judge the difference in capital cost.
- Consider the up-front charges as well as the capital cost.
- If you are tired, wait and go back when you are refreshed.
- If you are not sure about the reputation of a dealer, call your local Better Business Bureau.

WHAT TO LOOK FOR IN THE CONTRACT (REGULATION M)

Before you sign a lease contract, you should be sure that you understand it and that all the major terms of the agreement are covered. Fortunately for consumers, the government has provided help in the form of Regulation M, part of the federal Truth-in-Lending Act. The regulation's purpose is to assure that lessees of personal property are given meaningful disclosures of lease terms, that the ultimate liability of lessees is spelled out, and that advertisements meaningfully and accurately disclose lease terms.

Regulation M governs *consumer* leasing. It does not cover vehicles with a capital cost in excess of $25,000, nor does it cover corporate or professional leases. If your lease falls into one of the excluded categories, you should be very careful about the lease that you are signing. Basically these categories are not covered by any specific lease laws. If you are leasing an expensive car, take the time to make sure that Regulation M disclosures are on the lease anyway (it's likely they are). If the lease doesn't comply with Regulation M, you should probably not sign it without having your lawyer or accountant look at it.

Regulation M states that the following information must be in any lease, so read the contract carefully to make sure that these terms are covered:

Description of the Leased Property

Make sure that the description of the vehicle on the lease papers matches the vehicle that you will be driving. A proper vehicle description includes the following items:

Model year—model year of the leased car
Make—nameplate of the leased vehicle
Model—model of the leased vehicle
Vehicle identification number—17-digit number assigned to the vehicle

It's not a bad idea to match the vehicle identification numbers. You can see the vehicle identification number (VIN) on the dashboard of the car as you peer through the windshield, or it may be on the inside of the driver's door.

Residual

If you have an option to purchase, the purchase option should be stated on the contract. If you do not have this option, that fact should be stated as well. If you have a fixed purchase option, the contract would simply state a dollar amount you will spend if you purchase the car at lease termination, as follows:

Lease residual value—the dollar value of your option to purchase

The purchase option may be disclosed as a *formula*; if so, be sure that you understand the formula before you sign the contract. The typical phrasing of a purchase option formula would be as follows:

> PURCHASE OPTION: If the lessee is not in default under the lease, the lessee has the option to buy the vehicle at the end of this lease for the sum of:
> 1) The vehicle's then-wholesale value as indicated in the NADA official used-car guide, excluding excess-mileage charges, plus 5 percent of such value, plus,
> 2) Any unpaid amounts then or past due under this lease, plus,
> 3) Any official fees and taxes required to be paid relating to the sale of the vehicle.

Excess Wear and Tear

The lease should include a paragraph disclosing the source bank's definition of excess wear and tear. It should also disclose the mileage allowed per year (or per month) and the penalties, if any, for excess mileage. Thus, a wear-and-tear clause might include the following language:

> I (the lessee) agree at my expense to have the vehicle serviced in accordance with the manufacturer's recommendations, to maintain the vehicle in good running condition, and to have all necessary repairs made. Unless I obtain your written permission beforehand, I will not make any changes to the vehicle that will decrease its economic value or functional utility. Any changes made to the vehicle that cannot be removed without decreasing its economic value or func-

Shopping for a Lease 53

tional utility will become your (the lessor's) property when made. If you request, you may inspect the vehicle at any reasonable time.

I also agree that when I return the vehicle to you, it will be in good running order and condition. I agree not to expose the vehicle to excess wear and tear. If I do so, then I am in default under this lease. In addition, if I do not buy the vehicle at the scheduled end of the term of this lease, I agree to be liable for the amount you reasonably estimate it would cost to make all repairs to the vehicle that are not the result of normal wear and tear, whether or not you in your sole discretion actually make the repairs.

This charge includes but is not limited to the amount you estimate it would cost to replace:

1) Any tire not part of a matching set of five tires (or four tires with an emergency "doughnut" spare if initially equipped as such), any tire with less than $1/8$ inch of tread remaining at the shallowest point, or any tire with gouged, plugged, or cut sidewalls, or

2) Missing or dented parts, accessories, or adornments, including bumpers, jacks, ornamentation, antennas, hubcaps, chrome strips, rearview mirrors, radio and stereo components, or

3) Any parts that are not original manufacturer equipment or of equal quality and design or any and all other damage or defects in the glass, body, or interior beyond ordinary wear and tear.

I promise and you agree that if the amount you estimate as the cost to put the vehicle in good running condition exceeds $100, I will pay the difference.

This clause deserves a closer look. Its sheer length makes it seem foreboding, as if the lease bank is intent upon picking the returned car to death when it is returned. In fact, this is not the case. This example is one of the better-written wear-and-tear clauses because it outlines what is expected in a very detailed format and because it indicates a lack of interest in nickeling and diming the customer. Remember the first $100 of excess wear and tear are the responsibility of the lessor. The things that the bank asks to be in place are reasonable. A car with missing or damaged parts simply commands less as a used car than one that is in proper condition. The paragraph about tires may seem long and picky, but it all gets to the same thing. Would you want a used car with bald, unmatched tires?

Voluntary Early Termination

The disclosure section of the lease should include provisions for voluntary early termination, since Regulation M does not require that lessors spell out their formula for determining the price of early termination. Under Regulation M, it is acceptable to state only that "the lessee has no option to terminate early." In reality, lessors *will* give their lessees the right to terminate, but lessors are not required to disclose their formula for early termination in the lease. Here is an example of early termination provisions to be sure are in your lease:

> This lease may be terminated by the lessee before the end of the term if the lessee is not in default under this lease, gives the lessor 10 days' written notice, delivers the vehicle to the lessor, and pays to the lessor at once the following:
> 1) An early-termination fee of $200,
> 2) The difference, if any, between the adjusted balance subject to lease charges and the residualized value of the vehicle, and
> 3) All other amounts due under this lease.

If you are looking at a long-term lease, it is particularly important to read this clause, especially the costs involved. Because many banks do not officially disclose their formula for computing the cost of early termination, be sure to get those terms on a signed letterhead before you sign the lease.

Initial Charges

Your contract should provide a breakdown of all initial outlays. In most cases, the following items would be included:

Advance Monthly Payment—the amount of your monthly payment
Excise or Personal Property Tax—the tax amount if required or "N/A" if tax is not required
Refundable Security Deposit—an amount agreed upon when negotiating the lease; normally does not exceed one month's payment by more than $100
(This part of the lease should clearly state that the security deposit is "refundable.")
Registration and Other Fees—the cost of licensing the car, for example, property taxes, inspection fees, or any other local fees required
Total Payment Due at Inception—the total of all the preceding amounts

Payment Schedule

The lease should provide a payment schedule that specifies the term of the lease; the amount of each payment, including tax; the total of all payments; and the date each payment is due, as in the following example:

> The lessee agrees to pay (<u>term</u>) payments of $(<u>monthly amount</u>). The first payment is due on the date of this lease. The rest of the payments during the term of this lease are due on the 15th day of the month for the months following the first month. All the amounts that the lessee must pay under the lease, and that are not in the total monthly payment, will be paid directly by the lessee.
> 1) **Total of Basic Monthly Rentals:** *monthly amount not including tax × number of months in the term*
> 2) **Total of Monthly Payments:** *monthly amount including tax or any other monthly fee required*

Where tax is not the responsibility of the lessee, the amounts in (1) and (2) of the example should be identical.

Default Clause

In a default clause, the lease should disclose what constitutes a default of the lease, and what remedies are available to the lessee and lessor in case of default. The following example is typical:

> If the lessee fails to make any payment under this lease when it is due, or if the lessee fails to keep any other agreement in this lease, the lessor may terminate this lease and take back the vehicle. The lessor may go on the lessee's property to retake the vehicle. Even if the lessor retakes the vehicle, the lessee must still pay at once the sum of:
> 1) The difference, if any, between the adjusted balance, subject to lease charges and net amount received by the lessor upon the sale of the vehicle at wholesale, and
> 2) All other amounts then due under this lease. The lessee must also pay all expenses paid by the lessor to enforce the lessor's rights under this lease. This includes reasonable attorney fees as permitted by law, and any damage caused to the lessor because of the lessee's default. The lessor may sell the vehicle at public or private sale with or without the knowledge of the lessee.

Insurance Clause

The lease should indicate the levels of insurance necessary to keep the lease from being in default. It should also indicate whether the insurance is provided by the lessor. (In general today, it is not.) In reviewing the following sample insurance clause, keep in mind that the minimum levels of coverage will change from one lease bank to the next:

> The lessee must insure the vehicle with insurance companies acceptable to the lessor for the term of this lease and give the lessor proof of that insurance. This insurance must protect the lessee and the lessor. It must consist of:
> 1) Comprehensive fire and theft insurance with a deductible amount of not more than $500,
> 2) Collision and upset insurance with a deductible of not more than $500, and
> 3) Automobile liability and uninsured and underinsured

Shopping for a Lease 57

motorist insurance with limits of not less than $100,000 for any one person, $300,000 for any one accident, and $50,000 for property damage without deductible.
Vehicle insurance and/or liability insurance are not provided by the lessor.

Lease Termination Clause

The lease should provide a clear method for terminating the lease at lease-end. It should indicate what responsibilities the lessee has for returning the vehicle to an appropriate place and what fees, if any, the lessee must pay. The following sample clause is typical:

> I agree that if I do not purchase the vehicle as provided above, the amount that I owe you at the end of the lease term will be the sum of the following:
> 1) Any disposition charge as indicated above.
> 2) Any monthly lease payments due and unpaid and any other amounts and charges arising from my failure to keep my promises under this lease.
> 3) Any charge for excess mileage as provided for above.
> 4) The amount you must spend to put the car in good working condition as provided for above.

With regard to the disposition charge in item (1), many lease companies charge a lease-end fee to dispose of the car that you are returning.

Loss of Vehicle

Regulation M does *not require* that the lease contain a paragraph pertaining to loss or destruction of the vehicle, but a lessee should look for it. This paragraph outlines the lessee's responsibilities should the car be destroyed or stolen before lease-end. In general, look for your responsibilities to be identical to those you would have in an early termination. The following clause would be reasonable:

> If the vehicle is lost or destroyed and the lessee is not in default under this lease, the lessee may provide a substitute

vehicle, satisfactory to the lessor, and continue this lease. Any insurance proceeds paid with respect to the vehicle shall be applied to the purchase of the substitute vehicle. If the lessee does not provide a substitute vehicle, the lessee shall pay to the lessor the difference, if any, between:

1) The sum of the adjusted balance, subject to lease charges, and all other amounts then due under this lease.

2) The amount of insurance proceeds received by the lessor for the vehicle.

Concluding Thoughts About Regulation M

Regulation M is 51 pages long, and any consumer lease is required to have more disclosures than the ones outlined here. However, those mentioned in this section are the most important ones.

Remember, Regulation M does not protect lessees of expensive cars or corporate lessees. Therefore, it is especially important for those lessees to avoid an open-end lease. There is literally *no limit* to the back-end risk you take in that kind of lease. Also, if you are not automatically covered under Regulation M, it would be advisable for your lawyer or accountant to review a completed copy of the lease before you sign.

Finally, with rare exception, lease banks are unwilling to alter the body of their contracts. If a lease contains a phrase or condition that you cannot live with, move on to another bank. Do not attempt to get the bank to rewrite the contract.

WHAT TO LOOK FOR IN THE CONTRACT (REGULATION M)

- Regulation M is part of the federal Truth-in-Lending Act.
- It is designed to assure lessees that they receive complete and meaningful lease disclosures.
- Regulation M does not cover any car with a capital cost in excess of $25,000 or corporate and professional leases.
- Regulation M requires the disclosure of, among other things, description of the leased property, the residual value, definitions of excess wear and tear and excess mileage, a breakdown of initial charges, a payment schedule, definition of and remedies for default, required insurance coverage, and the method for termination at lease-end.
- Not required under Regulation M but advisable are clauses spelling out provisions for early termination and the lessee's responsibilities if the car is destroyed or stolen.
- If your type of lease is not covered under Regulation M, have it reviewed by your lawyer or accountant.
- Lease banks are reluctant to change their contracts, so find a bank whose contract is acceptable.

5
Buying Insurance

Insuring your leased car should not be much different from insuring the same car if it were purchased, but some differences do apply. Most lease banks require proof that the car is insured before the car is delivered, and they set minimum standards for that insurance. Typically the limits of liability must be at least $100,000 for any one person and $300,000 per accident. Liability for property damage would have to be covered to at least $50,000. The deductible for comprehensive coverage (insurance against fire, theft, and acts of God) can usually be set to a maximum of $500, but some lease banks require a deductible of $250 or less. The same is true for the collision deductible.

When you insure the leased car, the lease bank must be named as the loss payee and the additional insured. In rare cases, the bank may have separate names and addresses for the loss payee and additional insured, but that practice is in decline. To be sure that the right car is being insured and that the right people are being named in the policy, let the dealership's leasing personnel talk directly to the insurance company. At the same time, the dealership can confirm the insurance for the lease bank.

Since insurance is such a large part of the cost of operating a vehicle, it is smart to shop insurance rates just as you shopped for the best lease and lease rate. The differences can be staggering.

If your car is stolen or destroyed during the lease term, your insurance carrier is not necessarily going to pay the full amount that you would owe the bank at an early termination.

Most insurance contracts are written to pay the retail value of the missing automobile. If the car is brand-new (less than one year old), many insurance companies will pay for the cost of a new car minus a fixed amount per mile (assumed or proven). If the car is a little older, the payment amount will usually reflect the average retail cost of purchasing a like car.

Since the insurance company pays an amount set on a retail basis and the residual of your lease is set on a wholesale basis, the window of vulnerability is not nearly as large as it would be if you were trying to trade in your car early, yet there is still some risk. Several remedies are available that may reduce the risk.

The most recent tool to appear for leasing professionals is *gap insurance*. New York has recently become the first state to pass legislation *requiring* gap insurance, and other states may follow. This insurance policy can cost anywhere from 3 percent to 6 percent of the monthly payment. It is designed to make up the difference between the early-termination value and the insurance receipts in the case that the car is stolen or destroyed.

Gap insurance can be a good bet, especially when you are in a manufacturer's lease or you feel that the residual value is greater than the car should be worth, but be as careful shopping for this coverage as you are shopping for the best lease price. The price for the policy should be around $300 for the entire length of the contract. If gap insurance were costing substantially more than that, it would be the most expensive answer available to a lessee.

Not all gap insurance is alike. Some gap policies will pay only if the car is totaled in an accident, not if the car is stolen. This type of policy costs money but still leaves you vulnerable. In most cases, a car will not be destroyed or stolen during the lease term. In the few cases where loss does occur, many are settled without loss to the lessee.

More common is the practice of "rolling over" the difference into the next lease. The gap is made up by applying it to the next lease as additional capital cost. This would raise the monthly payment on the next lease.

Rarely used, but most effective in keeping the lease payments down, is *substitute collateral*. Many banks will let you continue the lease on the same schedule if you can find a car that is similar to the one that was lost. Since the insurance company will pay the retail replacement value, this means that you have no out-of-pocket expense to replace the car save the insurance deductible.

The best way to manage the gap is to avoid it altogether. Choose a car that does not have a reputation for being stolen. Also, avoid unnecessary "aftersale"—that is, usually overpriced and unnecessary products pitched to you after you sign the lease on your car—a remote alarm, undercoating, paint sealant, an extended warranty, or rustproofing, for example. (If you are keeping the car for five years or less, rustproofing is an unnecessary expense, and the insurance company will not pay for it in the case of a loss.)

Insurance once was commonly provided by the lease bank. The cost of the policy was simply folded into the lease payment. The banks were happy to do this because they would be sure that the leased car was insured. Today that kind of arrangement is still possible but rare. As insurance regulations became less uniform from state to state, the banks found it more and more difficult to find one policy that would fit all situations. As a result, the lease packages became uncompetitive.

Lease companies that do offer insurance may not have the best rates or terms. In addition, none can guarantee the cost of the insurance for the entire term. With such uncertainty, your lease rate will be sure to change every year. As a rule of thumb, built-in insurance raises your payment by $100 or more each month.

A better way to get insurance is to pick the best lease program without considering the insurance, then to pick the best insurance without considering the lease. You may even be able to pay for the insurance on a month-to-month basis. If that sounds unduly complicated, consider this analogy: When you buy a sound system, do you get better quality buying the best separate components or buying the prepackaged "system" at K mart?

BUYING INSURANCE

- Insurance on a leased car is not much different from that on a purchased car.
- The lease bank will require proof of insurance.
- The lease bank will set minimum insurance standards and stipulate that it be listed as loss payee and additional insured.
- Your insurance carrier may not pay the full amount of your obligation if the car is destroyed or stolen before the end of the lease.
- Two methods for dealing with this shortfall are to buy gap insurance or to roll over the difference into the next lease.
- The best way to manage the gap is to avoid it by choosing the right car.
- In general, lease banks and lease companies do not offer insurance as part of the lease.

6
Terminating Your Lease

The issues that arise when you terminate your lease depend in part on whether you wait until lease-end or seek to terminate the lease early. Also, in some cases you may want to buy your leased car or try to sell it yourself.

AT THE END OF THE LEASE TERM

If you are careful, concluding your lease at the end of the term can be painless. However, if you were careless about your choice of lease or the way you kept your car, you can be quite surprised when it comes time to turn the car back in. Without exception, a poorly kept car will cost a lessee money.

Open-End Leases

If a poorly kept car is part of an open-end lease, the lessee may have to come up with a tremendous amount of money. Even though Regulation M protects an individual in such leases by maximizing the lease-end payment at three times the monthly payment, it allows an exception if the lessor can prove excessive wear and tear.

Closed-End Leases

Most people reading this book will be interested in a closed-end lease. In such a lease, the customer is required to keep a car in good shape, excluding "average wear and tear."

At the start of the contract, you are asked to pay a security deposit. This amount (usually around one month's payment) is used as a reconditioning reserve at the time that the car comes off of lease. If the car has damage that exceeds the average wear and tear criteria of that lease bank, then the excess will be deducted from the security deposit before the deposit is returned to you. If the excess damage is greater than the security deposit, no money will be returned to you, and the lease bank will bill you for the amount outstanding.

As described in Chapter 4, most closed-end leases explicitly define excessive wear and tear in the contract. The lease will state that all the body parts should be present and free of dents and scratches. If there are scratches but they do not go through the paint, then these scratches may be buffed out and should not devalue the car. All mechanical parts should be operating. Power windows should go up and down, the air conditioner should work, and the transmission should still shift. The interior should not be physically damaged. Rips and cigarette burns are definitely excess wear and tear. Tires are generally required to have at least 25 percent of their life remaining. A car cannot be sold as used if the tires are bald.

If your car meets these conditions, there is no real need to worry. If it comes close, except perhaps a very small ding or two, there is also no reason for concern. However, we cannot pick the people who park next to us at the mall, nor those who might cause an accident while we have a car. In these cases, the car should be repaired before lease-end.

If the damage is great, such as in an accident, you should enter an insurance claim and have the car repaired so that it will measure up to the standards set forth in the lease. If the damage is less, but still significant such as a small dent or several deep scratches, spend the time to get these deficiencies corrected before you end the lease. You will probably pay less for the repairs when you can shop around, and your lessor will be more forgiving of smaller problems that would be borderline. Think of it this way: If you were selling this car, you would want to show it off in the best light. So do the lease banks that now have to dispose of your car.

> # AT THE END OF THE LEASE TERM
>
> - Ending the lease is easiest if you have taken good care of the car.
> - If the car has excess wear and tear, open-end leases are especially bad.
> - In a closed-end lease, you will not be responsible for average wear and tear.
> - The security deposit will help offset damages beyond average wear and tear.
> - The definition of "excess wear and tear" should be spelled out in the lease contract.

GETTING OUT OF YOUR LEASE EARLY

This book has discussed various strategies for leasing a car. Many of them succeed with careful planning and following through on those plans. However, from time to time, even the best laid plans go awry, so you might find yourself having to end a lease before you intended.

When you sign your name to a lease, make sure you understand the actions that will take place should you want to get out of your lease early. The dealer's statement "Don't worry, I'll take care of you when that time comes" is not an adequate description of an early-termination policy.

When you lease a car, your equity payments are far smaller than they would be if you were purchasing the car; after all, you are only paying the difference between the selling price and the residual value. In addition, in most cases you have not put any money down to offset the rapid depreciation that occurs when a car goes from being new to being used. This means that in the early stages of a lease, even in one charging level-yield interest, you would pay more money to get out of your contract than the car would be worth on any market.

If you sign a lease that does not spell out your early-termination options, see if the lease manager will sign a letter that will spell out those options; otherwise look for a different lessor. If a bank is looking for large penalty payments or charges most of the interest to the early years of the loan, you should carefully weigh the possibilities of terminating the lease early. Look at a manufacturer's lease only in terms of not terminating the lease. On this type of lease, the subsidized residual is so high that any early termination would be virtually unaffordable.

"Rolling It Over"

One way to end your lease early and not pay the amount you owe is to "roll it over" into the next lease. While this may result in no out-of-pocket expense, it certainly will result in higher monthly payments and an even more adverse position should you want to terminate early again.

As a rule of thumb, you can figure that in a five-year lease every $1,000 you roll over into the next lease will show up as a $20 increase in your payment on that lease. This translates to roughly $25 per month on a 48-month lease and $33 per month on a 36-month lease. A $3,000 deficit rolled over into a three-year lease could mean a payment boost of $100 per month.

Subleasing

One way that may be tempting you to get out of an "upside down" lease early—that is, a lease in which you owe more to the bank than the car can be sold for—is by subleasing. In subleasing, the lessee tries to get someone else to take over the lease where the lessee left off without notifying the lease bank. This effort is based on the lessee's belief that he or she can stop being responsible for the old car and move on to the new. Unfortunately, however, this is not true, since all leases and almost all states prohibit subleasing.

The reasons are myriad. First, a sublessee has not been screened for creditworthiness by the lease bank. The person to whom you sublease your car may not be in the habit of paying bills on time or perhaps at all. Once the sublessee has taken the car from you, you have lost control over the use or whereabouts of the car, but you're still responsible for the payments to the bank. If the money fails to arrive at the bank in a timely manner, there is no collateral to move against in order to satisfy the obligation.

Some companies advertise themselves as agents designed to find sublessees for your car. Resist the temptation! What they are doing is putting you at extreme risk, and it may take you a lifetime to make reparations.

Lease Assumption

There is one method similar to subleasing that works; it is called lease assumption. In this version of subleasing, the lease bank has agreed to look at the credit of a potential new lessee. If the credit is satisfactory, the bank will continue the lease with the new person and will leave you out of the loop. If you are not in direct contact with the lease bank, you are not doing a lease assumption.

Sometimes the lease bank will grant the new person the assumption only if you stay on the contract as a cosigner. Unless the new lessee is a close friend, you should avoid accepting cosigner status for all the reasons you would avoid a sublease. Work out every step directly with the bank, and be sure you know what your obligations will be down the road.

Lease assumption has one serious pitfall. It is difficult to find the right person to assume the lease. This person must be strong enough financially to lease a new car on his or her own. In addition, the new lessee must be willing to pay what amounts to a new-car payment for used-car value. Finding the right person could take tremendous patience.

Selling

Giving your leased vehicle back to the dealer before you planned to can compound an already bad situation. Cars depreciate far more in the first two years than they do in the last three years of a five-year lease. If you find yourself needing to end a lease before it reaches wholesale equity, your best bet is to sell the car on your own. This tactic is detailed in the following sections on how to buy your car and then tips on sure ways to sell it.

GETTING OUT OF YOUR LEASE EARLY

- Do not accept "don't worry about it" as an early-termination plan.
- Very early termination will result in being "upside down"—having to pay more to get out of the lease than your car is worth.
- Avoid leases with large early termination penalties.
- To end a lease early, you might "roll over" the amount you owe, applying it against the next lease.
- Subleasing is occasionally used but very risky and usually prohibited.
- Lease assumption is less risky but much more difficult.
- Your best bet is to buy the car and then sell it.

BUYING YOUR LEASED CAR

Under some circumstances, it is wise to buy your leased car at the end of the contract term. If you discover that you used considerably less mileage than the amount allowed by the lessor, or that the residual value (if fixed at the beginning of the lease) is actually below the market value of the car, buying the car and then selling it would put money in your pocket. In some cases, you might buy the vehicle to use as a second car or to avoid further indebtedness.

If you are interested in buying your leased vehicle, pay attention to the contract. You will pay the residual value when buying the car, if that amount is fixed, plus any applicable fees. Many lease companies charge a lease termination fee—even if you are purchasing the car! You will also have to pay tax and all registration costs so that the car can be titled in your name. Beyond that, you should have no further expenses.

Unfortunately, some people are all too willing to take advantage of your decision to buy. These unscrupulous dealers add "dealership fees" and "transfer fees" that are not spelled out in the lease contract. These fees amount to little more than added dealer profit and should not be tolerated—if they are imposed, ask to have them removed. If they are not removed, cite Regulation M as the governing ordinance in the lease contract (if your lease is a Reg M lease), and ask the dealer to show you where those fees are specified in the contract.

If you have a lease with a fair market value purchase option, Regulation M stipulates that a formula be in the contract that spells out the criteria used to establish "fair market value" at lease-end. Read this formula carefully to be sure that you understand it. For example, one lessee was ready to terminate her lease by purchasing her leased car at "fair market value." The lease stated that the value would be determined by averaging the wholesale and retail prices in the used-car guide of the lease bank's choice. These prices would be set as if the car had average wear and tear and the mileage allowed by the contract (72,000 miles were allowed in her contract). The customer was quoted the average of the retail and wholesale prices from the used car guide, but the dealer figured average was based on the car's actual mileage on the odometer—with 50,000 miles—an incorrect interpretation of the contract. This set her buyout price based on 72,000 miles on the car, no matter how many miles she actually used. (She would have had to pay more if she'd used *more* than 72,000 miles, however.) By the correct interpretation of her fair market value purchase option, then, she was able to purchase the car for $1,100 less than the original quote.

Understanding the arcane language of the lease contract may not be one of your innate talents. If you have an accountant or lawyer, you may want to ask his or her opinion before you write any checks.

BUYING YOUR LEASED CAR

- Buying your leased car can make sense if you have used far fewer miles than expected (so the value of the car is greater than the amount set in the purchase option), if the market value was underestimated (so the price for exercising the purchase option is less than the car's market value), or if you wish to avoid greater indebtedness.
- Your only expenses should be the residual value, lease termination fee (if any), tax, and registration costs.
- Watch out for unnecessary fees and charges, and ask to have them removed before you sign the contract.
- If you have an open-end lease, read the fair market value formula. Understanding this formula may save you hundreds of dollars.
- If you need help, consult a lawyer or accountant.

SELLING YOUR CAR

The only affordable way to terminate a lease early may be to find a buyer for the car. If you choose this approach, set aside a Sunday or two for potential customers to view and perhaps test-drive the car.

Create a newspaper ad listing every option that the car has. Do not satisfy yourself with catchall terms such as *loaded*. Keep in mind that the eventual buyer may know nothing about the car you are offering for sale. If you follow this tactic, you will create a larger and more informative ad. Although you may expect to pay more for a larger ad, it will stand out among the more mundane ads on either side, and it will be among the first ads potential buyers will respond to.

Use words that will attract the type of clientele your car will appeal to. Describe a European car as being in "pristine condition," but use "cream puff" for a cheap runabout.

Don't lie! If your ad is successful, you will attract people from varying distances. Be sure to be accurate in your description of the car, as people will not appreciate driving to your house on a false alarm.

Place your ad in a regional paper on Sunday only, rather than in your local paper several times a week. Someone in Staten Island who is interested in purchasing a used car will buy the *Staten Island Advance* on Sunday and the *New York Times*. Someone who lives on Long Island will buy *Newsday* and the *New York Times*. Someone in Hackensack will buy the *Bergen Record* and the *New York Times*. You are interested in reaching the widest audience possible for the quickest turnaround. Also, it behooves the papers to have you place your ad more than once a week, so many papers offer a two-day special. This does not work in your favor, because you'll be fielding phone calls and visits both days. You need only give up some Sundays, not the rest of the week.

When setting a price, be sure to step back from your car and see it as your customer would. As a start, use the NADA retail guide (available at the library). From the price there, deduct excess mileage, if any, per their excess-mileage chart. Then deduct the cost of repairing damage, if any. This leaves you with the retail value of the car on a used-car lot. Because you are not a dealer and you are selling this car "as is" to the new owner, you should not expect to realize full retail value. You may advertise the retail value and field offers for less, or you might choose to drop $500 from the retail value and advertise the price as "firm."

Finally, believe in your car. Of all the cars sold in the United States, you leased this one. It must hold some special charm for you. Be confident that the price you set is fair. If you are not confident about the product you choose or the price that the market has already established for the car of your choice, you will have a hard time convincing someone else of its value.

When you have found a buyer for your car, make sure that the deal is solid by securing a deposit, then arrange for the bank to be paid off. Some banks allow the new owner to pay them off, and most banks will be happy to put the title directly in the name of the new owner (so you avoid sales tax). Make sure you know the mechanics of the bank buyout before you have a deal, so that you can move quickly when the time comes.

Selling your car in the retail market is not necessary if you have already reached a wholesale equity point, since at that point you could trade in your car and owe nothing more to the bank. However, with the differences between retail and wholesale values, you may be interested in selling your car yourself anyway since your car could fetch much more in the retail market. If you can sell your car for $2,000 more than the residual value, you've put $2,000 in your pocket.

SELLING YOUR CAR

- Selling your car may be the only affordable way to terminate your lease early.
- Set aside a couple of Sundays for test drives.
- Place a newspaper ad that lists all of your car's options.
- Use words that are expected among the clientele you expect to attract.
- Do not lie.
- Place your ad in the Sunday paper only. If you can place it in a regional paper, instead of a local paper, do so.
- To set a price, use the NADA retail guide, but be sure to deduct for defects.
- Believe in your car. The belief is infectious.
- When you have found a buyer, secure your deal with a security deposit.
- The difference between wholesale and retail prices may make it worthwhile to sell your car even if you don't have to.

7
Answers to Your Questions on Leasing

Q: Why should I lease?
A: A lease contract will cost less than a finance contract for the same car and term unless you make a substantial down payment on a lease. (See Chapter 1.)

Most leases do not require any down payment. This saves your funds for paying other debts, starting a new project, or accumulating interest.

For the self-employed person or a corporation, a lease may offer tax advantages that are not available to purchasers of cars, as the cost of a leased car is tax deductible. (See the discussion of tax strategies in Chapter 3.)

A lease will allow the customer to make the largest payment at the end of the lease term and at the customer's option. This is the time when a customer will best know whether the car is worth the payment of the residual to buy the car.

Many manufacturers artificially support the residual values of the cars under their leases. (See the discussion of manufacturer's leases in Chapter 2.) Leasing these cars can result in both substantially lower monthly payments and total cost over the period of time normally associated with the sale.

High-mileage users can take advantage of the fact that an expensive car will depreciate more than the excess mileage fees cover, so that high-mileage drivers will get their money's worth. (See the discussion of the high-mileage strategy in Chapter 3.)

Leasing can make the car you desire fit into the budget

that you are living with. In other words, because monthly payments are lower, you will be able to drive a better model than you could if you were buying a car.

If you take care to choose the right lease, buying your car at lease-end can be *less* expensive than purchasing through traditional financing. (See the discussion of leasing to buy in Chapter 3.)

Q: Wait a second! If I take the monthly payment of a 60-month lease and multiply it by 60, I'll end up paying the same amount in the lease as I would pay if I bought the car, but in the lease I won't have the car at the end. How can a lease be cheaper?

A: Indeed, if you take the total of monthly payments for a long-term lease and compare it with the selling price, the lease payments would not seem favorable. But don't forget that money has value. That value always grows or has to be paid for. For example, $10,000.00 at 10 percent compounded annually for five years is worth $16,105.10. On these terms, someone who paid $10,000.00 cash for a car *lost* $6,105.10 in interest when his or her money went for the car instead of earning 10 percent interest. Someone who financed a purchase would have to pay a comparable amount in interest. So to compare values fairly, ask for a monthly finance amount on the same term, if you borrowed all of the principal. Multiply this figure by the term, and deduct your fair expectation of what you could get selling the car at lease term. (See the discussion of leasing to buy in Chapter 3.)

Q: Why do dealerships push leasing so much?

A: There are many reasons that a dealership encourages leasing. They may feel that leasing will make them more money in some cases. Other dealerships push it because it's new, but the most important reason is that a lease is often easier to sell than a new-car purchase. The price of an average new car has risen faster than the cost of living, making that car less and less affordable. The lease is one way of bringing that car back into a budget. Another reason is that differences in payments tend to trivialize the differences in price between two cars or dealerships. A customer might be more willing to travel back to another dealership to save $500 in the purchase price than to save a mere $10 per month in lease payments.

Also, the dealer's ability to sell a more expensive car is improved in a lease. Residual value makes the more expensive cars nearly as affordable as less expensive cars. The dealer's margin of profit is generally (but not always) higher on the more expensive cars, and the customer is more likely to become emotionally attached to a glamorous and expensive car.

Q: How do I know when I have a fair lease price?

A: Since lease residuals change from model to model and from bank to bank, there is no easy way of knowing that you are receiving the right price for the right car. The best method of determining the answer to the question takes some work. Submit the lease quote you have to the marketplace, and shop the lease quote from dealer to dealer. (See the section on finding the best deal in Chapter 4.) As an alternative method, you can use a pocket calculator and duplicate the formulas in Chapter 4's section on figuring the cost of a lease. If the monthly figures agree and you are satisfied that the interest rates, residual values, and capital costs are all competitive, then you will know that the lease quote is the right one for you.

This last method is definitely not for the uninitiated. The formulas are complex, and the average person may not be sure what a competitive residual or a good residual should be. While the formulas might be valuable to "keep the lease manager honest," you'll still discover the best monthly amount through comparison.

Q: My brother-in-law says the best way to get a lease is to negotiate a purchase price first and then to ask the dealer to convert it to a lease. Does that work?

A: That tactic is not recommended in shopping for a lease. While it is true that many dealerships are honest, others simply are not. This tactic is tailor-made for the latter category. A Smilin' Sammy can easily quote a price that is lower than the price he would need to make a deal and bump the selling price up when it comes time to figure out the lease. Even following the formulas in Chapter 4 will give you poor results. Smilin' Sammy can simply increase the interest rate to *show* a lower capital cost. Remember that in most states the lease contract need not disclose the selling price of the car.

The other weakness of this tactic is that it attacks the question of selling price without giving fair attention to the residual value of the automobile or the interest rate being charged. All three of these components need to be competitive in order for you to have a competitive lease quote. Using this tactic virtually ensures that you will end up doing business with the most outlandish liar you shop.

Q: I read the ads in the newspaper, but I never seem to be able to realize the deals when I follow them through. What am I doing wrong?

A: It's not what you are doing wrong, it's the nature of car advertising. The ads are fraught with inaccuracies and double meanings. They are not a very reliable source of honest information. Read Chapter 4.

Most state legislatures have done a lot to curb this kind of abuse, but as they become more clever in their enforcement, the dishonest car dealer can become more clever in making representations. Not too long ago, it was a general perception that car purchases were a matter of caveat emptor (let the buyer beware). With the complexity of even the most straightforward automobile transaction in this day, the assumption that buyers can protect themselves is eroded. The average person cannot possibly follow all of the calculations needed to protect his or her rights. Until the state legislatures can protect the consumer adequately, you will have to view newspaper ads with a great deal of skepticism.

Q: I heard that one of the advantages of leasing is that the lessor takes care of all the service and insurance. Is that true?

A: Some lessors do take service and insurance into consideration; they can usually put together special packages. These packages are not designed to be cost-competitive; rather, they are convenient.

The lease that takes all into account is relatively rare. For the most part, the lease you are shown when you visit the showroom is a simple closed-end lease with an option to purchase. The lease will not exempt you from amounts due on the servicing of your car or the insurance you must keep on it.

That is not such a terrible burden. If you combine a lease rate and insurance and extended service, you will receive a mediocre version of each one. If you shop for the best lease and the best insurance and purchase the best warranty (there are warranties that include standard maintenance), you will get a lot more value for your money.

Q: The lease manager always seems to be working with list price—can I get a lease that is not worked from list?

A: Leases are not all calculated from list price. However, the most common way to calculate the residual value is as a percentage of list price. Since the sale price of your particular car will not alter the used-car value at lease termination, the only consistent way a bank can place a residual value on each car is as a percentage of list price. The selling price to the bank may be at list price, and it may be higher than list.

This is also true of cars that are sold outright. However, if the car is regularly discounted when it is sold, it should also be discounted when leased, or the lease price will not be competitive with other lease prices available. (See Chapter 4.)

Q: I've heard about people being trapped in a lease that they no longer want. Shouldn't that make purchasing a safer investment?
A: Most leases are written without any money down. They are also written so that the only principal paid is the depreciation of the car. For this reason, leases can be expensive to terminate early. Whether you lease or purchase will not affect the quick depreciation of your new car. It is often this depreciation that makes extraction from a lease difficult. When you purchase a car, you are expected to come up with a large down payment. If you finance the balance, you will pay a larger monthly payment and thus more principal each month.

The combination of down payment and greater payments each month conspire to take some of the sting away from early termination of a finance contract, but we tend to forget that we lose the money we have already spent. The large down payment was lost on the very first day, and it was lost when it was worth the most (assuming any inflation rate). The consolation for early terminators is that while they owe more on the lease than the value of the car, the money they have to come up with is the cheapest possible money available (because it is paid later rather than sooner, so inflation has taken some value away).

Some lease contracts are especially hard to terminate. These include contracts that do not rebate unearned interest on an early termination and manufacturer's leases. To avoid the former, be sure to understand the early-termination provisions of your lease contract before you sign it. You should avoid the latter type of lease unless you are certain that you are comfortable with the length of the contract.

If you are looking for the most flexible terms for lease termination, be sure to pick a lease with a low residual (as in an ALG lease) and a level-yield formula for lease termination. The combination of these ingredients will give you the lowest payoff in an early termination—though not the lowest monthly payment. (See the discussion of long-term leases in Chapter 2.)

Q: I am a salesperson employed by a company to cover a large territory. Can I deduct my lease payments on my taxes?

A: Yes, unless your company already reimburses you, or they make the lease payments, in which case the company can deduct the payments as a business expense. You can deduct only the portion of the expenses that are related to business, however. (See the discussion of tax strategies in Chapter 3.)

Q: I would like to lease, but I am also attracted by those low interest rates that the manufacturer is offering on purchases. How do I choose?

A: Be sure to ask the dealership representative about special lease rates. It is rare that the manufacturer will have a special rate for financing and ignore the leasing part of the business. In addition, you may find that a lease with an outside bank may be more profitable if you elect to use the optional rebate that is often offered on such deals.

Chapter 2's discussion of manufacturer's leases covered the ramifications of the manufacturer subsidizing the residual value of the car. If these leases fit with your leasing criteria, they represent a far greater value to you than any rebate on a purchase.

Glossary

ALG lease: A lease in which the residual is an amount published in the *ALG Residual Percentage Guide*, available at most libraries. *ALG* stands for Automotive Lease Guide.
APR: Annual percentage rate; the rate of interest charged per year on the remaining balance of conventional financing. This rate is not generally used in leasing.
Assumption of a lease: An agreement between the lessee and lessor to allow a third party to take over the lease and to become the new lessee.
Back-end balloon: An amount of money due at the end of a lease, such as a buy-out figure.
Capital cost: The price—including sign-up fee and, in some cases, tax or other fees—that the lease bank pays to acquire the car.
Capital cost depreciator or **Capital cost reducer:** A down payment, trade-in, or anything paid at lease inception to reduce the capital cost of a leased vehicle. Also called a "front-end balloon."
Closed-end lease: A form of lease in which the dealer, instead of the customer, bears the risk that the value of the car at lease-end may be less than the residual value specified in the contract. Besides the payments specified in the contract, the customer is responsible only for compensating the dealer for excess mileage and excess wear and tear. The customer has no option to buy at the end of the lease unless such an option is stated in the contract.
Closed-end lease with option to buy: A closed-end lease in which a purchase option is stated as either a set dollar figure or a formula.
Depreciation: In a lease, the difference between the selling price (capital cost) and the residual value. In a

purchase, the difference between selling price and resale value.

Early termination: Ending a lease before the date originally agreed on in the lease contract.

Equity: The point where one's debt and assets (in leasing, the value of a leased car) are equal. *Wholesale equity* is the point at which the amount you owe on a lease equals the amount for which your car could be traded in. *Retail equity* is the point at which the amount you owe equals what your car could fetch if you sold it yourself.

Excess-mileage charge: The amount the lessee must pay for every mile over the contracted number. This usually ranges from 6 cents per mile to 15 cents per mile.

Fair market value purchase option: An option added to a lease to purchase a car for an amount determined by a formula set at lease inception.

Fixed purchase option: An option added to a lease to purchase a car for an amount fixed at lease inception.

Front-end balloon: *See* Capital cost depreciator.

Gap insurance: An insurance policy that pays the lease bank the difference between the early-termination value and the auto insurance reimbursement if the car is stolen or destroyed.

Investment tax credit (ITC): A tax credit on federal income taxes; designed to stimulate business investment in durable goods. For such capital expenditures, the business could subtract the credit from the amount of taxes it owed. This program was cancelled retroactive to January 1, 1986, but, who knows, it may one day make a reappearance.

Lease: A contract in which one person pays for the right to use an asset owned by another person.

Lease term: Period for which a lease is to be in effect.

Lessee: A lease customer; the person who makes payments for use of the leased item.

Lessor: Owner of a leased item.

Level-yield interest: An accounting formula that distributes the interest load evenly over the term.
Long-term lease: An auto lease for 60 months (five years).
Manufacturer's lease: An auto lease in which the manufacturer is the lessor. Usually the residual value is set high, making these leases expensive to terminate early.
MSRP: Manufacturer's suggested retail price (also called the list price). Most residual values are determined as a percentage of this figure.
NADA: The National Auto Dealers Association guides are the official used-car guides used by dealers and lease banks for current retail, wholesale, and loan values (the maximum amount a bank will loan for a particular car). NADA guides are available at libraries, banks, and insurance companies.
Open-end lease: A form of lease in which the value of the car is determined at lease-end. If this value is less than the residual value specified in the contract, the customer must make up the difference.
Regulation M: A part of the federal Truth-in-Lending Act requiring full and meaningful disclosure to lessees of personal property.
Residual value: The amount that the bank sets as the expected value of a vehicle at lease-end.
Retail equity: *See* Equity.
Security deposit: Amount that the lessee turns over to the lessor at the outset of a lease to secure the lessor against excessive wear and tear. Any amount not needed to repair excess wear and tear is returned to the lessee at lease-end.
Short-term lease: A lease that runs for 24 or 36 months.
Sign-up fee: A fixed amount of money, added to the capital cost of the car, charged by the bank to offset the expense of setting up the account and processing the paperwork.
Subleasing: A method of getting out of a lease early in which the lessee finds someone to take over his or her lease without notifying the lessor. All leases and almost all states

prohibit subleasing and it should certainly be avoided.
Sublessee: A person who takes over a lease for a lessee, although not officially, since the lessee is still responsible for the payments and the leased car.
Substitute collateral: A comparable car purchased to continue a lease when the leased car is destroyed or stolen.
Wholesale equity: *See* Equity.
Yield percentage rate: The rate of interest charged on capital cost plus residual value. It is based upon term, not year, and is extensively used in leasing.

MONTHLY PAYMENTS FOR 24-MONTH CONVENTIONAL LOANS

Loan Amt.	8.00%	8.25%	8.50%	8.75%	9.00%	9.25%	9.50%	9.75%
$ 500	22.61	22.67	22.73	22.79	22.84	22.90	22.96	23.01
1,000	45.23	45.34	45.46	45.57	45.68	45.80	45.91	46.03
1,500	67.84	68.01	68.18	68.36	68.53	68.70	68.87	69.04
2,000	90.45	90.68	90.91	91.14	91.37	91.60	91.83	92.06
2,500	113.07	113.35	113.64	113.93	114.21	114.50	114.79	115.07
3,000	135.68	136.02	136.37	136.71	137.05	137.40	137.74	138.09
3,500	158.30	158.69	159.09	159.50	159.90	160.30	160.70	161.10
4,000	180.91	181.37	181.82	182.28	182.74	183.20	183.66	184.12
4,500	203.52	204.04	204.55	205.07	205.58	206.10	206.62	207.13
5,000	226.14	226.71	227.28	227.85	228.42	229.00	229.57	230.15
5,500	248.75	249.38	250.01	250.64	251.27	251.90	252.53	253.16
6,000	271.36	272.05	272.73	273.42	274.11	274.80	275.49	276.18
6,500	293.98	294.72	295.46	296.21	296.95	297.70	298.44	299.19
7,000	316.59	317.39	318.19	318.99	319.79	320.60	321.40	322.21
7,500	339.20	340.06	340.92	341.78	342.64	343.50	344.36	345.22
8,000	361.82	362.73	363.65	364.56	365.48	366.40	367.32	368.24
8,500	384.43	385.40	386.37	387.35	388.32	389.30	390.27	391.25
9,000	407.05	408.07	409.10	410.13	411.16	412.20	413.23	414.27
9,500	429.66	430.74	431.83	432.92	434.01	435.10	436.19	437.28
10,000	452.27	453.41	454.56	455.70	456.85	458.00	459.14	460.30
10,500	474.89	476.08	477.28	478.49	479.69	480.90	482.10	483.31
11,000	497.50	498.76	500.01	501.27	502.53	503.79	505.06	506.33
11,500	520.11	521.43	522.74	524.06	525.37	526.69	528.02	529.34
12,000	542.73	544.10	545.47	546.84	548.22	549.59	550.97	552.36
12,500	565.34	566.77	568.20	569.63	571.06	572.49	573.93	575.37
13,000	587.95	589.44	590.92	592.41	593.90	595.39	596.89	598.39
13,500	610.57	612.11	613.65	615.20	616.74	618.29	619.85	621.40
14,000	633.18	634.78	636.38	637.98	639.59	641.19	642.80	644.41
14,500	655.80	657.45	659.11	660.77	662.43	664.09	665.76	667.43
15,000	678.41	680.12	681.84	683.55	685.27	686.99	688.72	690.44
15,500	701.02	702.79	704.56	706.34	708.11	709.89	711.67	713.46
16,000	723.64	725.46	727.29	729.12	730.96	732.79	734.63	736.47
16,500	746.25	748.13	750.02	751.91	753.80	755.69	757.59	759.49
17,000	768.86	770.80	772.75	774.69	776.64	778.59	780.55	782.50
17,500	791.48	793.47	795.47	797.48	799.48	801.49	803.50	805.52
18,000	814.09	816.15	818.20	820.26	822.33	824.39	826.46	828.53
18,500	836.70	838.82	840.93	843.05	845.17	847.29	849.42	851.55
19,000	859.32	861.49	863.66	865.83	868.01	870.19	872.38	874.56
19,500	881.93	884.16	886.39	888.62	890.85	893.09	895.33	897.58
20,000	904.55	906.83	909.11	911.40	913.69	915.99	918.29	920.59
20,500	927.16	929.50	931.84	934.19	936.54	938.89	941.25	943.61
21,000	949.77	952.17	954.57	956.97	959.38	961.79	964.20	966.62
21,500	972.39	974.84	977.30	979.76	982.22	984.69	987.16	989.64
22,000	995.00	997.51	1,000.02	1,002.54	1,005.06	1,007.59	1,010.12	1,012.65
22,500	1,017.61	1,020.18	1,022.75	1,025.33	1,027.91	1,030.49	1,033.08	1,035.67
23,000	1,040.23	1,042.85	1,045.48	1,048.11	1,050.75	1,053.39	1,056.03	1,058.68
23,500	1,062.84	1,065.52	1,068.21	1,070.90	1,073.59	1,076.29	1,078.99	1,081.70
24,000	1,085.45	1,088.19	1,090.94	1,093.68	1,096.43	1,099.19	1,101.95	1,104.71
24,500	1,108.07	1,110.86	1,113.66	1,116.47	1,119.28	1,122.09	1,124.91	1,127.73
25,000	1,130.68	1,133.53	1,136.39	1,139.25	1,142.12	1,144.99	1,147.86	1,150.74
25,500	1,153.30	1,156.21	1,159.12	1,162.04	1,164.96	1,167.89	1,170.82	1,173.76
26,000	1,175.91	1,178.88	1,181.85	1,184.82	1,187.80	1,190.79	1,193.78	1,196.77
26,500	1,198.52	1,201.55	1,204.58	1,207.61	1,210.65	1,213.69	1,216.73	1,219.79
27,000	1,221.14	1,224.22	1,227.30	1,230.39	1,233.49	1,236.59	1,239.69	1,242.80
27,500	1,243.75	1,246.89	1,250.03	1,253.18	1,256.33	1,259.49	1,262.65	1,265.81
28,000	1,266.36	1,269.56	1,272.76	1,275.96	1,279.17	1,282.39	1,285.61	1,288.83
28,500	1,288.98	1,292.23	1,295.49	1,298.75	1,302.02	1,305.29	1,308.56	1,311.84
29,000	1,311.59	1,314.90	1,318.21	1,321.53	1,324.86	1,328.19	1,331.52	1,334.86
29,500	1,334.21	1,337.57	1,340.94	1,344.32	1,347.70	1,351.09	1,354.48	1,357.87
30,000	1,356.82	1,360.24	1,363.67	1,367.10	1,370.54	1,373.99	1,377.43	1,380.89
30,500	1,379.43	1,382.91	1,386.40	1,389.89	1,393.38	1,396.89	1,400.39	1,403.90
31,000	1,402.05	1,405.58	1,409.13	1,412.67	1,416.23	1,419.79	1,423.35	1,426.92
31,500	1,424.66	1,428.25	1,431.85	1,435.46	1,439.07	1,442.69	1,446.31	1,449.93
32,000	1,447.27	1,450.92	1,454.58	1,458.24	1,461.91	1,465.59	1,469.26	1,472.95
32,500	1,469.89	1,473.60	1,477.31	1,481.03	1,484.75	1,488.48	1,492.22	1,495.96
33,000	1,492.50	1,496.27	1,500.04	1,503.81	1,507.60	1,511.38	1,515.18	1,518.98
33,500	1,515.11	1,518.94	1,522.77	1,526.60	1,530.44	1,534.28	1,538.14	1,541.99
34,000	1,537.73	1,541.61	1,545.49	1,549.38	1,553.28	1,557.18	1,561.09	1,565.01
34,500	1,560.34	1,564.28	1,568.22	1,572.17	1,576.12	1,580.08	1,584.05	1,588.02
35,000	1,582.96	1,586.95	1,590.95	1,594.95	1,598.97	1,602.98	1,607.01	1,611.04

MONTHLY PAYMENTS FOR 24-MONTH CONVENTIONAL LOANS

Loan Amt.	10.00%	10.25%	10.50%	10.75%	11.00%	11.25%	11.50%	11.75%
$ 500	23.07	23.13	23.19	23.25	23.30	23.36	23.42	23.48
1,000	46.14	46.26	46.38	46.49	46.61	46.72	46.84	46.96
1,500	69.22	69.39	69.56	69.74	69.91	70.09	70.26	70.44
2,000	92.29	92.52	92.75	92.98	93.22	93.45	93.68	93.91
2,500	115.36	115.65	115.94	116.23	116.52	116.81	117.10	117.39
3,000	138.43	138.78	139.13	139.48	139.82	140.17	140.52	140.87
3,500	161.51	161.91	162.32	162.72	163.13	163.53	163.94	164.35
4,000	184.58	185.04	185.50	185.97	186.43	186.90	187.36	187.83
4,500	207.65	208.17	208.69	209.21	209.74	210.26	210.78	211.31
5,000	230.72	231.30	231.88	232.46	233.04	233.62	234.20	234.78
5,500	253.80	254.43	255.07	255.71	256.34	256.98	257.62	258.26
6,000	276.87	277.56	278.26	278.95	279.65	280.34	281.04	281.74
6,500	299.94	300.69	301.44	302.20	302.95	303.71	304.46	305.22
7,000	323.01	323.82	324.63	325.44	326.25	327.07	327.88	328.70
7,500	346.09	346.95	347.82	348.69	349.56	350.43	351.30	352.18
8,000	369.16	370.08	371.01	371.93	372.86	373.79	374.72	375.65
8,500	392.23	393.21	394.20	395.18	396.17	397.15	398.14	399.13
9,000	415.30	416.34	417.38	418.43	419.47	420.52	421.56	422.61
9,500	438.38	439.47	440.57	441.67	442.77	443.88	444.98	446.09
10,000	461.45	462.60	463.76	464.92	466.08	467.24	468.40	469.57
10,500	484.52	485.73	486.95	488.16	489.38	490.60	491.82	493.05
11,000	507.59	508.86	510.14	511.41	512.09	513.96	515.24	516.52
11,500	530.67	531.99	533.32	534.66	535.99	537.33	538.66	540.00
12,000	553.74	555.12	556.51	557.90	559.29	560.69	562.08	563.48
12,500	576.81	578.25	579.70	581.15	582.60	584.05	585.50	586.96
13,000	599.88	601.39	602.89	604.39	605.90	607.41	608.92	610.44
13,500	622.96	624.52	626.08	627.64	629.21	630.77	632.34	633.92
14,000	646.03	647.65	649.26	650.89	652.51	654.14	655.76	657.40
14,500	669.10	670.78	672.45	674.13	675.81	677.50	679.18	680.87
15,000	692.17	693.91	695.64	697.38	699.12	700.86	702.60	704.35
15,500	715.25	717.04	718.83	720.62	722.42	724.22	726.02	727.83
16,000	738.32	740.17	742.02	743.87	745.73	747.58	749.45	751.31
16,500	761.39	763.30	765.20	767.12	769.03	770.95	772.87	774.79
17,000	784.46	786.43	788.39	790.36	792.33	794.31	796.29	798.27
17,500	807.54	809.56	811.58	813.61	815.64	817.67	819.71	821.74
18,000	830.61	832.69	834.77	836.85	838.94	841.03	843.13	845.22
18,500	853.68	855.82	857.96	860.10	862.25	864.39	866.55	868.70
19,000	876.75	878.95	881.14	883.35	885.55	887.76	889.97	892.18
19,500	899.83	902.08	904.33	906.59	908.85	911.12	913.39	915.66
20,000	922.90	925.21	927.52	929.84	932.16	934.48	936.81	939.14
20,500	945.97	948.34	950.71	953.08	955.46	957.84	960.23	962.61
21,000	969.04	971.47	973.90	976.33	978.76	981.20	983.65	986.09
21,500	992.12	994.60	997.08	999.57	1,002.07	1,004.57	1,007.07	1,009.57
22,000	1,015.19	1,017.73	1,020.27	1,022.82	1,025.37	1,027.93	1,030.49	1,033.05
22,500	1,038.26	1,040.86	1,043.46	1,046.07	1,048.68	1,051.29	1,053.91	1,056.53
23,000	1,061.33	1,063.99	1,066.65	1,069.31	1,071.98	1,074.65	1,077.33	1,080.01
23,500	1,084.41	1,087.12	1,089.84	1,092.56	1,095.28	1,098.01	1,100.75	1,103.49
24,000	1,107.48	1,110.25	1,113.02	1,115.80	1,118.59	1,121.38	1,124.17	1,126.96
24,500	1,130.55	1,133.38	1,136.21	1,139.05	1,141.89	1,144.74	1,147.59	1,150.44
25,000	1,153.62	1,156.51	1,159.40	1,162.30	1,165.20	1,168.10	1,171.01	1,173.92
25,500	1,176.70	1,179.64	1,182.59	1,185.54	1,188.50	1,191.46	1,194.43	1,197.40
26,000	1,199.77	1,202.77	1,205.78	1,208.79	1,211.80	1,214.82	1,217.85	1,220.88
26,500	1,222.84	1,225.90	1,228.97	1,232.03	1,235.11	1,238.19	1,241.27	1,244.36
27,000	1,245.91	1,249.03	1,252.15	1,255.28	1,258.41	1,261.55	1,264.69	1,267.83
27,500	1,268.99	1,272.16	1,275.34	1,278.53	1,281.72	1,284.91	1,288.11	1,291.31
28,000	1,292.06	1,295.29	1,298.53	1,301.77	1,305.02	1,308.27	1,311.53	1,314.79
28,500	1,315.13	1,318.42	1,321.72	1,325.02	1,328.32	1,331.63	1,334.95	1,338.27
29,000	1,338.20	1,341.55	1,344.91	1,348.26	1,351.63	1,355.00	1,358.37	1,361.75
29,500	1,361.28	1,364.68	1,368.09	1,371.51	1,374.93	1,378.36	1,381.79	1,385.23
30,000	1,384.35	1,387.81	1,391.28	1,394.76	1,398.24	1,401.72	1,405.21	1,408.70
30,500	1,407.42	1,410.94	1,414.47	1,418.00	1,421.54	1,425.08	1,428.63	1,432.18
31,000	1,430.49	1,434.07	1,437.66	1,441.25	1,444.84	1,448.44	1,452.05	1,455.66
31,500	1,453.57	1,457.20	1,460.85	1,464.49	1,468.15	1,471.81	1,475.47	1,479.14
32,000	1,476.64	1,480.33	1,484.03	1,487.74	1,491.45	1,495.17	1,498.89	1,502.62
32,500	1,499.71	1,503.46	1,507.22	1,510.99	1,514.75	1,518.53	1,522.31	1,526.10
33,000	1,522.78	1,526.59	1,530.41	1,534.23	1,538.06	1,541.89	1,545.73	1,549.57
33,500	1,545.86	1,549.72	1,553.60	1,557.48	1,561.36	1,565.25	1,569.15	1,573.05
34,000	1,568.93	1,572.85	1,576.79	1,580.72	1,584.67	1,588.62	1,592.57	1,596.53
34,500	1,592.00	1,595.98	1,599.97	1,603.97	1,607.97	1,611.98	1,615.99	1,620.01
35,000	1,615.07	1,619.11	1,623.16	1,627.21	1,631.27	1,635.34	1,639.41	1,643.49

MONTHLY PAYMENTS FOR 24-MONTH CONVENTIONAL LOANS

Loan Amt.	12.00%	12.25%	12.50%	12.75%	13.00%	13.25%	13.50%	13.75%
$ 500	23.54	23.60	23.65	23.71	23.77	23.83	23.89	23.95
1,000	47.07	47.19	47.31	47.42	47.54	47.66	47.78	47.89
1,500	70.61	70.79	70.96	71.14	71.31	71.49	71.67	71.84
2,000	94.15	94.38	94.61	94.85	95.08	95.32	95.55	95.79
2,500	117.68	117.98	118.27	118.56	118.85	119.15	119.44	119.74
3,000	141.22	141.57	141.92	142.27	142.63	142.98	143.33	143.68
3,500	164.76	165.17	165.58	165.99	166.40	166.81	167.22	167.63
4,000	188.29	188.76	189.23	189.70	190.17	190.64	191.11	191.58
4,500	211.83	212.36	212.88	213.41	213.94	214.47	215.00	215.53
5,000	235.37	235.95	236.54	237.12	237.71	238.30	238.89	239.47
5,500	258.90	259.55	260.19	260.83	261.48	262.13	262.77	263.42
6,000	282.44	283.14	283.84	284.55	285.25	285.96	286.66	287.37
6,500	305.98	306.74	307.50	308.26	309.02	309.79	310.55	311.32
7,000	329.51	330.33	331.15	331.97	332.79	333.62	334.44	335.26
7,500	353.05	353.93	354.80	355.68	356.56	357.45	358.33	359.21
8,000	376.59	377.52	378.46	379.40	380.33	381.27	382.22	383.16
8,500	400.12	401.12	402.11	403.11	404.11	405.10	406.10	407.11
9,000	423.66	424.71	425.77	426.82	427.88	428.93	429.99	431.05
9,500	447.20	448.31	449.42	450.53	451.65	452.76	453.88	455.00
10,000	470.73	471.90	473.07	474.24	475.42	476.59	477.77	478.95
10,500	494.27	495.50	496.73	497.96	499.19	500.42	501.66	502.90
11,000	517.81	519.09	520.38	521.67	522.96	524.25	525.55	526.84
11,500	541.34	542.69	544.03	545.38	546.73	548.08	549.44	550.79
12,000	564.88	566.28	567.69	569.09	570.50	571.91	573.32	574.74
12,500	588.42	589.88	591.34	592.81	594.27	595.74	597.21	598.69
13,000	611.96	613.47	615.00	616.52	618.04	619.57	621.10	622.63
13,500	635.49	637.07	638.65	640.23	641.81	643.40	644.99	646.58
14,000	659.03	660.66	662.30	663.94	665.59	667.23	668.88	670.53
14,500	682.57	684.26	685.96	687.65	689.36	691.06	692.77	694.48
15,000	706.10	707.85	709.61	711.37	713.13	714.89	716.66	718.42
15,500	729.64	731.45	733.26	735.08	736.90	738.72	740.54	742.37
16,000	753.18	755.04	756.92	758.79	760.67	762.55	764.43	766.32
16,500	776.71	778.64	780.57	782.50	784.44	786.38	788.32	790.27
17,000	800.25	802.24	804.22	806.22	808.21	810.21	812.21	814.21
17,500	823.79	825.83	827.88	829.93	831.98	834.04	836.10	838.16
18,000	847.32	849.43	851.53	853.64	855.75	857.87	859.99	862.11
18,500	870.86	873.02	875.19	877.35	879.52	881.70	883.87	886.05
19,000	894.40	896.62	898.84	901.07	903.29	905.53	907.76	910.00
19,500	917.93	920.21	922.49	924.78	927.07	929.36	931.65	933.95
20,000	941.47	943.81	946.15	948.49	950.84	953.19	955.54	957.90
20,500	965.01	967.40	969.80	972.20	974.61	977.02	979.43	981.84
21,000	988.54	991.00	993.45	995.91	998.38	1,000.85	1,003.32	1,005.79
21,500	1,012.08	1,014.59	1,017.11	1,019.63	1,022.15	1,024.68	1,027.21	1,029.74
22,000	1,035.62	1,038.19	1,040.76	1,043.34	1,045.92	1,048.51	1,051.09	1,053.69
22,500	1,059.15	1,061.78	1,064.41	1,067.05	1,069.69	1,072.34	1,074.98	1,077.63
23,000	1,082.69	1,085.38	1,088.07	1,090.76	1,093.46	1,096.16	1,098.87	1,101.58
23,500	1,106.23	1,108.97	1,111.72	1,114.48	1,117.23	1,119.99	1,122.76	1,125.53
24,000	1,129.76	1,132.57	1,135.38	1,138.19	1,141.00	1,143.82	1,146.65	1,149.48
24,500	1,153.30	1,156.16	1,159.03	1,161.90	1,164.77	1,167.65	1,170.54	1,173.42
25,000	1,176.84	1,179.76	1,182.68	1,185.61	1,188.55	1,191.48	1,194.43	1,197.37
25,500	1,200.37	1,203.35	1,206.34	1,209.32	1,212.32	1,215.31	1,218.31	1,221.32
26,000	1,223.91	1,226.95	1,229.99	1,233.04	1,236.09	1,239.14	1,242.20	1,245.27
26,500	1,247.45	1,250.54	1,253.64	1,256.75	1,259.86	1,262.97	1,266.09	1,269.21
27,000	1,270.98	1,274.14	1,277.30	1,280.46	1,283.63	1,286.80	1,289.98	1,293.16
27,500	1,294.52	1,297.73	1,300.95	1,304.17	1,307.40	1,310.63	1,313.87	1,317.11
28,000	1,318.06	1,321.33	1,324.60	1,327.89	1,331.17	1,334.46	1,337.76	1,341.06
28,500	1,341.59	1,344.92	1,348.26	1,351.60	1,354.94	1,358.29	1,361.64	1,365.00
29,000	1,365.13	1,368.52	1,371.91	1,375.31	1,378.71	1,382.12	1,385.53	1,388.95
29,500	1,388.67	1,392.11	1,395.57	1,399.02	1,402.48	1,405.95	1,409.42	1,412.90
30,000	1,412.20	1,415.71	1,419.22	1,422.73	1,426.25	1,429.78	1,433.31	1,436.85
30,500	1,435.74	1,439.30	1,442.87	1,446.45	1,450.03	1,453.61	1,457.20	1,460.79
31,000	1,459.28	1,462.90	1,466.53	1,470.16	1,473.80	1,477.44	1,481.09	1,484.74
31,500	1,482.81	1,486.49	1,490.18	1,493.87	1,497.57	1,501.27	1,504.98	1,508.69
32,000	1,506.35	1,510.09	1,513.83	1,517.58	1,521.34	1,525.10	1,528.86	1,532.64
32,500	1,529.89	1,533.68	1,537.49	1,541.30	1,545.11	1,548.93	1,552.75	1,556.58
33,000	1,553.42	1,557.28	1,561.14	1,565.01	1,568.88	1,572.76	1,576.64	1,580.53
33,500	1,576.96	1,580.88	1,584.79	1,588.72	1,592.65	1,596.59	1,600.53	1,604.48
34,000	1,600.50	1,604.47	1,608.45	1,612.43	1,616.42	1,620.42	1,624.42	1,628.43
34,500	1,624.03	1,628.07	1,632.10	1,636.14	1,640.19	1,644.25	1,648.31	1,652.37
35,000	1,647.57	1,651.66	1,655.76	1,659.86	1,663.96	1,668.08	1,672.20	1,676.32

MONTHLY PAYMENTS FOR 36-MONTH CONVENTIONAL LOANS

Loan Amt.	8.00%	8.25%	8.50%	8.75%	9.00%	9.25%	9.50%	9.75%
$ 500	15.67	15.73	15.78	15.84	15.90	15.96	16.02	16.07
1,000	31.34	31.45	31.57	31.68	31.80	31.92	32.03	32.15
1,500	47.00	47.18	47.35	47.53	47.70	47.87	48.05	48.22
2,000	62.67	62.90	63.14	63.37	63.60	63.83	64.07	64.30
2,500	78.34	78.63	78.92	79.21	79.50	79.79	80.08	80.37
3,000	94.01	94.36	94.70	95.05	95.40	95.75	96.10	96.45
3,500	109.68	110.08	110.49	110.89	111.30	111.71	112.12	112.52
4,000	125.35	125.81	126.27	126.73	127.20	127.66	128.13	128.60
4,500	141.01	141.53	142.05	142.58	143.10	143.62	144.15	144.67
5,000	156.68	157.26	157.84	158.42	159.00	159.58	160.16	160.75
5,500	172.35	172.99	173.62	174.26	174.90	175.54	176.18	176.82
6,000	188.02	188.71	189.41	190.10	190.80	191.50	192.20	192.90
6,500	203.69	204.44	205.19	205.94	206.70	207.46	208.21	208.97
7,000	219.35	220.16	220.97	221.78	222.60	223.41	224.23	225.05
7,500	235.02	235.89	236.76	237.63	238.50	239.37	240.25	241.12
8,000	250.69	251.61	252.54	253.47	254.40	255.33	256.26	257.20
8,500	266.36	267.34	268.32	269.31	270.30	271.29	272.28	273.27
9,000	282.03	283.07	284.11	285.15	286.20	287.25	288.30	289.35
9,500	297.70	298.79	299.89	300.99	302.10	303.20	304.31	305.42
10,000	313.36	314.52	315.68	316.84	318.00	319.16	320.33	321.50
10,500	329.03	330.24	331.46	332.68	333.90	335.12	336.35	337.57
11,000	344.70	345.97	347.24	348.52	349.80	351.08	352.36	353.65
11,500	360.37	361.70	363.03	364.36	365.70	367.04	368.38	369.72
12,000	376.04	377.42	378.81	380.20	381.60	382.99	384.40	385.80
12,500	391.70	393.15	394.59	396.04	397.50	398.95	400.41	401.87
13,000	407.37	408.87	410.38	411.89	413.40	414.91	416.43	417.95
13,500	423.04	424.60	426.16	427.73	429.30	430.87	432.44	434.02
14,000	438.71	440.33	441.95	443.57	445.20	446.83	448.46	450.10
14,500	454.38	456.05	457.73	459.41	461.10	462.79	464.48	466.17
15,000	470.05	471.78	473.51	475.25	477.00	478.74	480.49	482.25
15,500	485.71	487.50	489.30	491.09	492.90	494.70	496.51	498.32
16,000	501.38	503.23	505.08	506.94	508.80	510.66	512.53	514.40
16,500	517.05	518.96	520.86	522.78	524.70	526.62	528.54	530.47
17,000	532.72	534.68	536.65	538.62	540.60	542.58	544.56	546.55
17,500	548.39	550.41	552.43	554.46	556.50	558.53	560.58	562.62
18,000	564.05	566.13	568.22	570.30	572.40	574.49	576.59	578.70
18,500	579.72	581.86	584.00	586.14	588.30	590.45	592.61	594.77
19,000	595.39	597.58	599.78	601.99	604.19	606.41	608.63	610.85
19,500	611.06	613.31	615.57	617.83	620.09	622.37	624.64	626.92
20,000	626.73	629.04	631.35	633.67	635.99	638.32	640.66	643.00
20,500	642.40	644.76	647.13	649.51	651.89	654.28	656.68	659.07
21,000	658.06	660.49	662.92	665.35	667.79	670.24	672.69	675.15
21,500	673.73	676.21	678.70	681.20	683.69	686.20	688.71	691.22
22,000	689.40	691.94	694.49	697.04	699.59	702.16	704.72	707.30
22,500	705.07	707.67	710.27	712.88	715.49	718.11	720.74	723.37
23,000	720.74	723.39	726.05	728.72	731.39	734.07	736.76	739.45
23,500	736.40	739.12	741.84	744.56	747.29	750.03	752.77	755.52
24,000	752.07	754.84	757.62	760.40	763.19	765.99	768.79	771.60
24,500	767.74	770.57	773.40	776.25	779.09	781.95	784.81	787.67
25,000	783.41	786.30	789.19	792.09	794.99	797.91	800.82	803.75
25,500	799.08	802.02	804.97	807.93	810.89	813.86	816.84	819.82
26,000	814.75	817.75	820.76	823.77	826.79	829.82	832.86	835.90
26,500	830.41	833.47	836.54	839.61	842.69	845.78	848.87	851.97
27,000	846.08	849.20	852.32	855.45	858.59	861.74	864.89	868.05
27,500	861.75	864.93	868.11	871.30	874.49	877.70	880.91	884.12
28,000	877.42	880.65	883.89	887.14	890.39	893.65	896.92	900.20
28,500	893.09	896.38	899.67	902.98	906.29	909.61	912.94	916.27
29,000	908.75	912.10	915.46	918.82	922.19	925.57	928.96	932.35
29,500	924.42	927.83	931.24	934.66	938.09	941.53	944.97	948.42
30,000	940.09	943.55	947.03	950.51	953.99	957.49	960.99	964.50
30,500	955.76	959.28	962.81	966.35	969.89	973.44	977.00	980.57
31,000	971.43	975.01	978.59	982.19	985.79	989.40	993.02	996.65
31,500	987.10	990.73	994.38	998.03	1,001.69	1,005.36	1,009.04	1,012.72
32,000	1,002.76	1,006.46	1,010.16	1,013.87	1,017.59	1,021.32	1,025.05	1,028.80
32,500	1,018.43	1,022.18	1,025.94	1,029.71	1,033.49	1,037.28	1,041.07	1,044.87
33,000	1,034.10	1,037.91	1,041.73	1,045.56	1,049.39	1,053.24	1,057.09	1,060.95
33,500	1,049.77	1,053.64	1,057.51	1,061.40	1,065.29	1,069.19	1,073.10	1,077.02
34,000	1,065.44	1,069.36	1,073.30	1,077.24	1,081.19	1,085.15	1,089.12	1,093.10
34,500	1,081.10	1,085.09	1,089.08	1,093.08	1,097.09	1,101.11	1,105.14	1,109.17
35,000	1,096.77	1,100.81	1,104.86	1,108.92	1,112.99	1,117.07	1,121.15	1,125.25

MONTHLY PAYMENTS FOR 36-MONTH CONVENTIONAL LOANS

Loan Amt.	10.00%	10.25%	10.50%	10.75%	11.00%	11.25%	11.50%	11.75%
$ 500	16.13	16.19	16.25	16.31	16.37	16.43	16.49	16.55
1,000	32.27	32.38	32.50	32.62	32.74	32.86	32.98	33.10
1,500	48.40	48.58	48.75	48.93	49.11	49.29	49.46	49.64
2,000	64.53	64.77	65.00	65.24	65.48	65.71	65.95	66.19
2,500	80.67	80.96	81.26	81.55	81.85	82.14	82.44	82.74
3,000	96.80	97.15	97.51	97.86	98.22	98.57	98.93	99.29
3,500	112.94	113.35	113.76	114.17	114.59	115.00	115.42	115.83
4,000	129.07	129.54	130.01	130.48	130.95	131.43	131.90	132.38
4,500	145.20	145.73	146.26	146.79	147.32	147.86	148.39	148.93
5,000	161.34	161.92	162.51	163.10	163.69	164.29	164.88	165.48
5,500	177.47	178.12	178.76	179.41	180.06	180.71	181.37	182.02
6,000	193.60	194.31	195.01	195.72	196.43	197.14	197.86	198.57
6,500	209.74	210.50	211.27	212.03	212.80	213.57	214.34	215.12
7,000	225.87	226.69	227.52	228.34	229.17	230.00	230.83	231.67
7,500	242.00	242.89	243.77	244.65	245.54	246.43	247.32	248.21
8,000	258.14	259.08	260.02	260.96	261.91	262.86	263.81	264.76
8,500	274.27	275.27	276.27	277.27	278.28	279.29	280.30	281.31
9,000	290.40	291.46	292.52	293.58	294.65	295.72	296.78	297.86
9,500	306.54	307.65	308.77	309.89	311.02	312.14	313.27	314.40
10,000	322.67	323.85	325.02	326.20	327.39	328.57	329.76	330.95
10,500	338.81	340.04	341.28	342.51	343.76	345.00	346.25	347.50
11,000	354.94	356.23	357.53	358.82	360.13	361.43	362.74	364.05
11,500	371.07	372.42	373.78	375.14	376.50	377.86	379.22	380.59
12,000	387.21	388.62	390.03	391.45	392.86	394.29	395.71	397.14
12,500	403.34	404.81	406.28	407.76	409.23	410.72	412.20	413.69
13,000	419.47	421.00	422.53	424.07	425.60	427.14	428.69	430.24
13,500	435.61	437.19	438.78	440.38	441.97	443.57	445.18	446.78
14,000	451.74	453.39	455.03	456.69	458.34	460.00	461.66	463.33
14,500	467.87	469.58	471.29	473.00	474.71	476.43	478.15	479.88
15,000	484.01	485.77	487.54	489.31	491.08	492.86	494.64	496.43
15,500	500.14	501.96	503.79	505.62	507.45	509.29	511.13	512.97
16,000	516.27	518.16	520.04	521.93	523.82	525.72	527.62	529.52
16,500	532.41	534.35	536.29	538.24	540.19	542.14	544.10	546.07
17,000	548.54	550.54	552.54	554.55	556.56	558.57	560.59	562.62
17,500	564.68	566.73	568.79	570.86	572.93	575.00	577.08	579.16
18,000	580.81	582.92	585.04	587.17	589.30	591.43	593.57	595.71
18,500	596.94	599.12	601.30	603.48	605.67	607.86	610.06	612.26
19,000	613.08	615.31	617.55	619.79	622.04	624.29	626.54	628.81
19,500	629.21	631.50	633.80	636.10	638.40	640.72	643.03	645.35
20,000	645.34	647.69	650.05	652.41	654.77	657.14	659.52	661.90
20,500	661.48	663.89	666.30	668.72	671.14	673.57	676.01	678.45
21,000	677.61	680.08	682.55	685.03	687.51	690.00	692.50	695.00
21,500	693.74	696.27	698.80	701.34	703.88	706.43	708.98	711.54
22,000	709.88	712.46	715.05	717.65	720.25	722.86	725.47	728.09
22,500	726.01	728.66	731.30	733.96	736.62	739.29	741.96	744.64
23,000	742.15	744.85	747.56	750.27	752.99	755.72	758.45	761.19
23,500	758.28	761.04	763.81	766.58	769.36	772.15	774.94	777.73
24,000	774.41	777.23	780.06	782.89	785.73	788.57	791.42	794.28
24,500	790.55	793.42	796.31	799.20	802.10	805.00	807.91	810.83
25,000	806.68	809.62	812.56	815.51	818.47	821.43	824.40	827.38
25,500	822.81	825.81	828.81	831.82	834.84	837.86	840.89	843.92
26,000	838.95	842.00	845.06	848.13	851.21	854.29	857.38	860.47
26,500	855.08	858.19	861.31	864.44	867.58	870.72	873.86	877.02
27,000	871.21	874.39	877.57	880.75	883.95	887.15	890.35	893.57
27,500	887.35	890.58	893.82	897.06	900.31	903.57	906.84	910.11
28,000	903.48	906.77	910.07	913.37	916.68	920.00	923.33	926.66
28,500	919.61	922.96	926.32	929.68	933.05	936.43	939.82	943.21
29,000	935.75	939.16	942.57	945.99	949.42	952.86	956.30	959.76
29,500	951.88	955.35	958.82	962.30	965.79	969.29	972.79	976.30
30,000	968.02	971.54	975.07	978.61	982.16	985.72	989.28	992.85
30,500	984.15	987.73	991.32	994.92	998.53	1,002.15	1,005.77	1,009.40
31,000	1,000.28	1,003.93	1,007.58	1,011.23	1,014.90	1,018.57	1,022.26	1,025.95
31,500	1,016.42	1,020.12	1,023.83	1,027.54	1,031.27	1,035.00	1,038.74	1,042.49
32,000	1,032.55	1,036.31	1,040.08	1,043.85	1,047.64	1,051.43	1,055.23	1,059.04
32,500	1,048.68	1,052.50	1,056.33	1,060.16	1,064.01	1,067.86	1,071.72	1,075.59
33,000	1,064.82	1,068.69	1,072.58	1,076.47	1,080.38	1,084.29	1,088.21	1,092.14
33,500	1,080.95	1,084.89	1,088.83	1,092.79	1,096.75	1,100.72	1,104.70	1,108.68
34,000	1,097.08	1,101.08	1,105.08	1,109.10	1,113.12	1,117.15	1,121.18	1,125.23
34,500	1,113.22	1,117.27	1,121.33	1,125.41	1,129.49	1,133.57	1,137.67	1,141.78
35,000	1,129.35	1,133.46	1,137.59	1,141.72	1,145.86	1,150.00	1,154.16	1,158.33

MONTHLY PAYMENTS FOR 36-MONTH CONVENTIONAL LOANS

Loan Amt.	12.00%	12.25%	12.50%	12.75%	13.00%	13.25%	13.50%	13.75%
$ 500	16.61	16.67	16.73	16.79	16.85	16.91	16.97	17.03
1,000	33.21	33.33	33.45	33.57	33.69	33.81	33.94	34.06
1,500	49.82	50.00	50.18	50.36	50.54	50.72	50.90	51.08
2,000	66.43	66.67	66.91	67.15	67.39	67.63	67.87	68.11
2,500	83.04	83.33	83.63	83.93	84.23	84.54	84.84	85.14
3,000	99.64	100.00	100.36	100.72	101.08	101.44	101.81	102.17
3,500	116.25	116.67	117.09	117.51	117.93	118.35	118.77	119.20
4,000	132.86	133.34	133.81	134.29	134.78	135.26	135.74	136.23
4,500	149.46	150.00	150.54	151.08	151.62	152.17	152.71	153.25
5,000	166.07	166.67	167.27	167.87	168.47	169.07	169.68	170.28
5,500	182.68	183.34	183.99	184.66	185.32	185.98	186.64	187.31
6,000	199.29	200.00	200.72	201.44	202.16	202.89	203.61	204.34
6,500	215.89	216.67	217.45	218.23	219.01	219.79	220.58	221.37
7,000	232.50	233.34	234.18	235.02	235.86	236.70	237.55	238.39
7,500	249.11	250.00	250.90	251.80	252.70	253.61	254.51	255.42
8,000	265.71	266.67	267.63	268.59	269.55	270.52	271.48	272.45
8,500	282.32	283.34	284.36	285.38	286.40	287.42	288.45	289.48
9,000	298.93	300.00	301.08	302.16	303.25	304.33	305.42	306.51
9,500	315.54	316.67	317.81	318.95	320.09	321.24	322.39	323.54
10,000	332.14	333.34	334.54	335.74	336.94	338.14	339.35	340.56
10,500	348.75	350.01	351.26	352.52	353.79	355.05	356.32	357.59
11,000	365.36	366.67	367.99	369.31	370.63	371.96	373.29	374.62
11,500	381.96	383.34	384.72	386.10	387.48	388.87	390.26	391.65
12,000	398.57	400.01	401.44	402.88	404.33	405.77	407.22	408.68
12,500	415.18	416.67	418.17	419.67	421.17	422.68	424.19	425.70
13,000	431.79	433.34	434.90	436.46	438.02	439.59	441.16	442.73
13,500	448.39	450.01	451.62	453.24	454.87	456.50	458.13	459.76
14,000	465.00	466.67	468.35	470.03	471.72	473.40	475.09	476.79
14,500	481.61	483.34	485.08	486.82	488.56	490.31	492.06	493.82
15,000	498.21	500.01	501.80	503.60	505.41	507.22	509.03	510.84
15,500	514.82	516.67	518.53	520.39	522.26	524.12	526.00	527.87
16,000	531.43	533.34	535.26	537.18	539.10	541.03	542.96	544.90
16,500	548.04	550.01	551.98	553.97	555.95	557.94	559.93	561.93
17,000	564.64	566.68	568.71	570.75	572.80	574.85	576.90	578.96
17,500	581.25	583.34	585.44	587.54	589.64	591.75	593.87	595.99
18,000	597.86	600.01	602.17	604.33	606.49	608.66	610.84	613.01
18,500	614.46	616.68	618.89	621.11	623.34	625.57	627.80	630.04
19,000	631.07	633.34	635.62	637.90	640.19	642.48	644.77	647.07
19,500	647.68	650.01	652.35	654.69	657.03	659.38	661.74	664.10
20,000	664.29	666.68	669.07	671.47	673.88	676.29	678.71	681.13
20,500	680.89	683.34	685.80	688.26	690.73	693.20	695.67	698.15
21,000	697.50	700.01	702.53	705.05	707.57	710.10	712.64	715.18
21,500	714.11	716.68	719.25	721.83	724.42	727.01	729.61	732.21
22,000	730.71	733.34	735.98	738.62	741.27	743.92	746.58	749.24
22,500	747.32	750.01	752.71	755.41	758.11	760.83	763.54	766.27
23,000	763.93	766.68	769.43	772.19	774.96	777.73	780.51	783.30
23,500	780.54	783.35	786.16	788.98	791.81	794.64	797.48	800.32
24,000	797.14	800.01	802.89	805.77	808.65	811.55	814.45	817.35
24,500	813.75	816.68	819.61	822.55	825.50	828.46	831.41	834.38
25,000	830.36	833.35	836.34	839.34	842.35	845.36	848.38	851.41
25,500	846.96	850.01	853.07	856.13	859.20	862.27	865.35	868.44
26,000	863.57	866.68	869.79	872.92	876.04	879.18	882.32	885.46
26,500	880.18	883.35	886.52	889.70	892.89	896.08	899.29	902.49
27,000	896.79	900.01	903.25	906.49	909.74	912.99	916.25	919.52
27,500	913.39	916.68	919.97	923.28	926.58	929.90	933.22	936.55
28,000	930.00	933.35	936.70	940.06	943.43	946.81	950.19	953.58
28,500	946.61	950.01	953.43	956.85	960.28	963.71	967.16	970.61
29,000	963.21	966.68	970.16	973.64	977.12	980.62	984.12	987.63
29,500	979.82	983.35	986.88	990.42	993.97	997.53	1,001.09	1,004.66
30,000	996.43	1,000.02	1,003.61	1,007.21	1,010.82	1,014.43	1,018.06	1,021.69
30,500	1,013.04	1,016.68	1,020.34	1,024.00	1,027.67	1,031.34	1,035.03	1,038.72
31,000	1,029.64	1,033.35	1,037.06	1,040.78	1,044.51	1,048.25	1,051.99	1,055.75
31,500	1,046.25	1,050.02	1,053.79	1,057.57	1,061.36	1,065.16	1,068.96	1,072.77
32,000	1,062.86	1,066.68	1,070.52	1,074.36	1,078.21	1,082.06	1,085.93	1,089.80
32,500	1,079.47	1,083.35	1,087.24	1,091.14	1,095.05	1,098.97	1,102.90	1,106.83
33,000	1,096.07	1,100.02	1,103.97	1,107.93	1,111.90	1,115.88	1,119.86	1,123.86
33,500	1,112.68	1,116.68	1,120.70	1,124.72	1,128.75	1,132.79	1,136.83	1,140.89
34,000	1,129.29	1,133.35	1,137.42	1,141.50	1,145.59	1,149.69	1,153.80	1,157.92
34,500	1,145.89	1,150.02	1,154.15	1,158.29	1,162.44	1,166.60	1,170.77	1,174.94
35,000	1,162.50	1,166.68	1,170.88	1,175.08	1,179.29	1,183.51	1,187.74	1,191.97

MONTHLY PAYMENTS FOR 48-MONTH CONVENTIONAL LOANS

Loan Amt.	8.00%	8.25%	8.50%	8.75%	9.00%	9.25%	9.50%	9.75%
$ 500	12.21	12.27	12.32	12.38	12.44	12.50	12.56	12.62
1,000	24.41	24.53	24.65	24.77	24.89	25.00	25.12	25.24
1,500	36.62	36.80	36.97	37.15	37.33	37.51	37.68	37.86
2,000	48.83	49.06	49.30	49.53	49.77	50.01	50.25	50.49
2,500	61.03	61.33	61.62	61.92	62.21	62.51	62.81	63.11
3,000	73.24	73.59	73.94	74.30	74.66	75.01	75.37	75.73
3,500	85.45	85.86	86.27	86.68	87.10	87.51	87.93	88.35
4,000	97.65	98.12	98.59	99.07	99.54	100.02	100.49	100.97
4,500	109.86	110.39	110.92	111.45	111.98	112.52	113.05	113.59
5,000	122.06	122.65	123.24	123.83	124.43	125.02	125.62	126.21
5,500	134.27	134.92	135.57	136.22	136.87	137.52	138.18	138.83
6,000	146.48	147.18	147.89	148.60	149.31	150.02	150.74	151.46
6,500	158.68	159.45	160.21	160.98	161.75	162.53	163.30	164.08
7,000	170.89	171.71	172.54	173.37	174.20	175.03	175.86	176.70
7,500	183.10	183.98	184.86	185.75	186.64	187.53	188.42	189.32
8,000	195.30	196.24	197.19	198.13	199.08	200.03	200.99	201.94
8,500	207.51	208.51	209.51	210.52	211.52	212.53	213.55	214.56
9,000	219.72	220.77	221.83	222.90	223.97	225.04	226.11	227.18
9,500	231.92	233.04	234.16	235.28	236.41	237.54	238.67	239.81
10,000	244.13	245.30	246.48	247.67	248.85	250.04	251.23	252.43
10,500	256.34	257.57	258.81	260.05	261.29	262.54	263.79	265.05
11,000	268.54	269.83	271.13	272.43	273.74	275.04	276.35	277.67
11,500	280.75	282.10	283.46	284.81	286.18	287.55	288.92	290.29
12,000	292.96	294.37	295.78	297.20	298.62	300.05	301.48	302.91
12,500	305.16	306.63	308.10	309.58	311.06	312.55	314.04	315.53
13,000	317.37	318.90	320.43	321.96	323.51	325.05	326.60	328.15
13,500	329.57	331.16	332.75	334.35	335.95	337.55	339.16	340.78
14,000	341.78	343.43	345.08	346.73	348.39	350.05	351.72	353.40
14,500	353.99	355.69	357.40	359.11	360.83	362.56	364.29	366.02
15,000	366.19	367.96	369.72	371.50	373.28	375.06	376.85	378.64
15,500	378.40	380.22	382.05	383.88	385.72	387.56	389.41	391.26
16,000	390.61	392.49	394.37	396.26	398.16	400.06	401.97	403.88
16,500	402.81	404.75	406.70	408.65	410.60	412.56	414.53	416.50
17,000	415.02	417.02	419.02	421.03	423.05	425.07	427.09	429.13
17,500	427.23	429.28	431.35	433.41	435.49	437.57	439.65	441.75
18,000	439.43	441.55	443.67	445.80	447.93	450.07	452.22	454.37
18,500	451.64	453.81	455.99	458.18	460.37	462.57	464.78	466.99
19,000	463.85	466.08	468.32	470.56	472.82	475.07	477.34	479.61
19,500	476.05	478.34	480.64	482.95	485.26	487.58	489.90	492.23
20,000	488.26	490.61	492.97	495.33	497.70	500.08	502.46	504.85
20,500	500.46	502.87	505.29	507.71	510.14	512.58	515.02	517.48
21,000	512.67	515.14	517.61	520.10	522.59	525.08	527.59	530.10
21,500	524.88	527.40	529.94	532.48	535.03	537.58	540.15	542.72
22,000	537.08	539.67	542.26	544.86	547.47	550.09	552.71	555.34
22,500	549.29	551.93	554.59	557.25	559.91	562.59	565.27	567.96
23,000	561.50	564.20	566.91	569.63	572.36	575.09	577.83	580.58
23,500	573.70	576.47	579.24	582.01	584.80	587.59	590.39	593.20
24,000	585.91	588.73	591.56	594.40	597.24	600.09	602.96	605.82
24,500	598.12	601.00	603.88	606.78	609.68	612.60	615.52	618.45
25,000	610.32	613.26	616.21	619.16	622.13	625.10	628.08	631.07
25,500	622.53	625.53	628.53	631.55	634.57	637.60	640.64	643.69
26,000	634.74	637.79	640.86	643.93	647.01	650.10	653.20	656.31
26,500	646.94	650.06	653.18	656.31	659.45	662.60	665.76	668.93
27,000	659.15	662.32	665.50	668.70	671.90	675.11	678.32	681.55
27,500	671.36	674.59	677.83	681.08	684.34	687.61	690.89	694.17
28,000	683.56	686.85	690.15	693.46	696.78	700.11	703.45	706.80
28,500	695.77	699.12	702.48	705.85	709.22	712.61	716.01	719.42
29,000	707.97	711.38	714.80	718.23	721.67	725.11	728.57	732.04
29,500	720.18	723.65	727.12	730.61	734.11	737.62	741.13	744.66
30,000	732.39	735.91	739.45	743.00	746.55	750.12	753.69	757.28
30,500	744.59	748.18	751.77	755.38	758.99	762.62	766.26	769.90
31,000	756.80	760.44	764.10	767.76	771.44	775.12	778.82	782.52
31,500	769.01	772.71	776.42	780.14	783.88	787.62	791.38	795.14
32,000	781.21	784.97	788.75	792.53	796.32	800.13	803.94	807.77
32,500	793.42	797.24	801.07	804.91	808.76	812.63	816.50	820.39
33,000	805.63	809.50	813.39	817.29	821.21	825.13	829.06	833.01
33,500	817.83	821.77	825.72	829.68	833.65	837.63	841.63	845.63
34,000	830.04	834.04	838.04	842.06	846.09	850.13	854.19	858.25
34,500	842.25	846.30	850.37	854.44	858.53	862.64	866.75	870.87
35,000	854.45	858.57	862.69	866.83	870.98	875.14	879.31	883.49

MONTHLY PAYMENTS FOR 48-MONTH CONVENTIONAL LOANS

Loan Amt.	10.00%	10.25%	10.50%	10.75%	11.00%	11.25%	11.50%	11.75%
$ 500	12.68	12.74	12.80	12.86	12.92	12.98	13.04	13.11
1,000	25.36	25.48	25.60	25.72	25.85	25.97	26.09	26.21
1,500	38.04	38.22	38.41	38.59	38.77	38.95	39.13	39.32
2,000	50.73	50.97	51.21	51.45	51.69	51.93	52.18	52.42
2,500	63.41	63.71	64.01	64.31	64.61	64.92	65.22	65.53
3,000	76.09	76.45	76.81	77.17	77.54	77.90	78.27	78.63
3,500	88.77	89.19	89.61	90.03	90.46	90.88	91.31	91.74
4,000	101.45	101.93	102.41	102.90	103.38	103.87	104.36	104.85
4,500	114.13	114.67	115.22	115.76	116.30	116.85	117.40	117.95
5,000	126.81	127.41	128.02	128.62	129.23	129.84	130.45	131.06
5,500	139.49	140.16	140.82	141.48	142.15	142.82	143.49	144.16
6,000	152.18	152.90	153.62	154.35	155.07	155.80	156.53	157.27
6,500	164.86	165.64	166.42	167.21	168.00	168.79	169.58	170.37
7,000	177.54	178.38	179.22	180.07	180.92	181.77	182.62	183.48
7,500	190.22	191.12	192.03	192.93	193.84	194.75	195.67	196.58
8,000	202.90	203.86	204.83	205.79	206.76	207.74	208.71	209.69
8,500	215.58	216.60	217.63	218.66	219.69	220.72	221.76	222.80
9,000	228.26	229.35	230.43	231.52	232.61	233.70	234.80	235.90
9,500	240.94	242.09	243.23	244.38	245.53	246.69	247.85	249.01
10,000	253.63	254.83	256.03	257.24	258.46	259.67	260.89	262.11
10,500	266.31	267.57	268.84	270.10	271.38	272.65	273.93	275.22
11,000	278.99	280.31	281.64	282.97	284.30	285.64	286.98	288.32
11,500	291.67	293.05	294.44	295.83	297.22	298.62	300.02	301.43
12,000	304.35	305.79	307.24	308.69	310.15	311.61	313.07	314.54
12,500	317.03	318.54	320.04	321.55	323.07	324.50	326.11	327.64
13,000	329.71	331.28	332.84	334.42	335.99	337.57	339.16	340.75
13,500	342.39	344.02	345.65	347.28	348.91	350.56	352.20	353.85
14,000	355.08	356.76	358.45	360.14	361.84	363.54	365.25	366.96
14,500	367.76	369.50	371.25	373.00	374.76	376.52	378.29	380.06
15,000	380.44	382.24	384.05	385.86	387.68	389.51	391.34	393.17
15,500	393.12	394.98	396.85	398.73	400.61	402.49	404.38	406.27
16,000	405.80	407.73	409.65	411.59	413.53	415.47	417.42	419.38
16,500	418.48	420.47	422.46	424.45	426.45	428.46	430.47	432.49
17,000	431.16	433.21	435.26	437.31	439.37	441.44	443.51	445.59
17,500	443.85	445.95	448.06	450.17	452.30	454.42	456.56	458.70
18,000	456.53	458.69	460.86	463.04	465.22	467.41	469.60	471.80
18,500	469.21	471.43	473.66	475.90	478.14	480.39	482.65	484.91
19,000	481.89	484.17	486.46	488.76	491.06	493.37	495.69	498.01
19,500	494.57	496.91	499.27	501.62	503.99	506.36	508.74	511.12
20,000	507.25	509.66	512.07	514.49	516.91	519.34	521.78	524.23
20,500	519.93	522.40	524.87	527.35	529.83	532.33	534.82	537.33
21,000	532.61	535.14	537.67	540.21	542.76	545.31	547.87	550.44
21,500	545.30	547.88	550.47	553.07	555.68	558.29	560.91	563.54
22,000	557.98	560.62	563.27	565.93	568.60	571.28	573.96	576.65
22,500	570.66	573.36	576.08	578.80	581.52	584.26	587.00	589.75
23,000	583.34	586.10	588.88	591.66	594.45	597.24	600.05	602.86
23,500	596.02	598.85	601.68	604.52	607.37	610.23	613.09	615.96
24,000	608.70	611.59	614.48	617.38	620.29	623.21	626.14	629.07
24,500	621.38	624.33	627.28	630.24	633.22	636.19	639.18	642.18
25,000	634.06	637.07	640.08	643.11	646.14	649.18	652.23	655.28
25,500	646.75	649.81	652.89	655.97	659.06	662.16	665.27	668.39
26,000	659.43	662.55	665.69	668.83	671.98	675.14	678.31	681.49
26,500	672.11	675.29	678.49	681.69	684.91	688.13	691.36	694.60
27,000	684.79	688.04	691.29	694.56	697.83	701.11	704.40	707.70
27,500	697.47	700.78	704.09	707.42	710.75	714.10	717.45	720.81
28,000	710.15	713.52	716.89	720.28	723.67	727.08	730.49	733.92
28,500	722.83	726.26	729.70	733.14	736.60	740.06	743.54	747.02
29,000	735.51	739.00	742.50	746.00	749.52	753.05	756.58	760.13
29,500	748.20	751.74	755.30	758.87	762.44	766.03	769.63	773.23
30,000	760.88	764.48	768.10	771.73	775.37	779.01	782.67	786.34
30,500	773.56	777.23	780.90	784.59	788.29	792.00	795.71	799.44
31,000	786.24	789.97	793.70	797.45	801.21	804.98	808.76	812.55
31,500	798.92	802.71	806.51	810.31	814.13	817.96	821.80	825.65
32,000	811.60	815.45	819.31	823.18	827.06	830.95	834.85	838.76
32,500	824.28	828.19	832.11	836.04	839.98	843.93	847.89	851.87
33,000	836.97	840.93	844.91	848.90	852.90	856.91	860.94	864.97
33,500	849.65	853.67	857.71	861.76	865.83	869.90	873.98	878.08
34,000	862.33	866.42	870.51	874.63	878.75	882.88	887.03	891.18
34,500	875.01	879.16	883.32	887.49	891.67	895.86	900.07	904.29
35,000	887.69	891.90	896.12	900.35	904.59	908.85	913.12	917.39

MONTHLY PAYMENTS FOR 48-MONTH CONVENTIONAL LOANS

Loan Amt.	12.00%	12.25%	12.50%	12.75%	13.00%	13.25%	13.50%	13.75%
$ 500	13.17	13.23	13.29	13.35	13.41	13.48	13.54	13.60
1,000	26.33	26.46	26.58	26.70	26.83	26.95	27.08	27.20
1,500	39.50	39.69	39.87	40.06	40.24	40.43	40.61	40.80
2,000	52.67	52.91	53.16	53.41	53.65	53.90	54.15	54.40
2,500	65.83	66.14	66.45	66.76	67.07	67.38	67.69	68.00
3,000	79.00	79.37	79.74	80.11	80.48	80.86	81.23	81.60
3,500	92.17	92.60	93.03	93.46	93.90	94.33	94.77	95.20
4,000	105.34	105.83	106.32	106.81	107.31	107.81	108.31	108.80
4,500	118.50	119.06	119.61	120.17	120.72	121.28	121.84	122.41
5,000	131.67	132.28	132.90	133.52	134.14	134.76	135.38	136.01
5,500	144.84	145.51	146.19	146.87	147.55	148.23	148.92	149.61
6,000	158.00	158.74	159.48	160.22	160.96	161.71	162.46	163.21
6,500	171.17	171.97	172.77	173.57	174.38	175.19	176.00	176.81
7,000	184.34	185.20	186.06	186.93	187.79	188.66	189.53	190.41
7,500	197.50	198.43	199.35	200.28	201.21	202.14	203.07	204.01
8,000	210.67	211.65	212.64	213.63	214.62	215.61	216.61	217.61
8,500	223.84	224.88	225.93	226.98	228.03	229.09	230.15	231.21
9,000	237.00	238.11	239.22	240.33	241.45	242.57	243.69	244.81
9,500	250.17	251.34	252.51	253.68	254.86	256.04	257.23	258.41
10,000	263.34	264.57	265.80	267.04	268.27	269.52	270.76	272.01
10,500	276.51	277.80	279.09	280.39	281.69	282.99	284.30	285.61
11,000	289.67	291.02	292.38	293.74	295.10	296.47	297.84	299.21
11,500	302.84	304.25	305.67	307.09	308.52	309.95	311.38	312.81
12,000	316.01	317.48	318.96	320.44	321.93	323.42	324.92	326.41
12,500	329.17	330.71	332.25	333.79	335.34	336.90	338.45	340.02
13,000	342.34	343.94	345.54	347.15	348.76	350.37	351.99	353.62
13,500	355.51	357.17	358.83	360.50	362.17	363.85	365.53	367.22
14,000	368.67	370.39	372.12	373.85	375.58	377.32	379.07	380.82
14,500	381.84	383.62	385.41	387.20	389.00	390.80	392.61	394.42
15,000	395.01	396.85	398.70	400.55	402.41	404.28	406.14	408.02
15,500	408.17	410.08	411.99	413.91	415.83	417.75	419.68	421.62
16,000	421.34	423.31	425.28	427.26	429.24	431.23	433.22	435.22
16,500	434.51	436.54	438.57	440.61	442.65	444.70	446.76	448.82
17,000	447.68	449.76	451.86	453.96	456.07	458.18	460.30	462.42
17,500	460.84	462.99	465.15	467.31	469.48	471.66	473.84	476.02
18,000	474.01	476.22	478.44	480.66	482.89	485.13	487.37	489.62
18,500	487.18	489.45	491.73	494.02	496.31	498.61	500.91	503.22
19,000	500.34	502.68	505.02	507.37	509.72	512.08	514.45	516.82
19,500	513.51	515.91	518.31	520.72	523.14	525.56	527.99	530.42
20,000	526.68	529.14	531.60	534.07	536.55	539.03	541.53	544.02
20,500	539.84	542.36	544.89	547.42	549.96	552.51	555.06	557.63
21,000	553.01	555.59	558.18	560.78	563.38	565.99	568.60	571.23
21,500	566.18	568.82	571.47	574.13	576.79	579.46	582.14	584.83
22,000	579.34	582.05	584.76	587.48	590.20	592.94	595.68	598.43
22,500	592.51	595.28	598.05	600.83	603.62	606.41	609.22	612.03
23,000	605.68	608.51	611.34	614.18	617.03	619.89	622.76	625.63
23,500	618.85	621.73	624.63	627.53	630.45	633.37	636.29	639.23
24,000	632.01	634.96	637.92	640.89	643.86	646.84	649.83	652.83
24,500	645.18	648.19	651.21	654.24	657.27	660.32	663.37	666.43
25,000	658.35	661.42	664.50	667.59	670.69	673.79	676.91	680.03
25,500	671.51	674.65	677.79	680.94	684.10	687.27	690.45	693.63
26,000	684.68	687.88	691.08	694.29	697.51	700.75	703.98	707.23
26,500	697.85	701.10	704.37	707.64	710.93	714.22	717.52	720.83
27,000	711.01	714.33	717.66	721.00	724.34	727.70	731.06	734.43
27,500	724.18	727.56	730.95	734.35	737.76	741.17	744.60	748.03
28,000	737.35	740.79	744.24	747.70	751.17	754.65	758.14	761.63
28,500	750.51	754.02	757.53	761.05	764.58	768.12	771.68	775.24
29,000	763.68	767.25	770.82	774.40	778.00	781.60	785.21	788.84
29,500	776.85	780.47	784.11	787.76	791.41	795.08	798.75	802.44
30,000	790.02	793.70	797.40	801.11	804.82	808.55	812.29	816.04
30,500	803.18	806.93	810.69	814.46	818.24	822.03	825.83	829.64
31,000	816.35	820.16	823.98	827.81	831.65	835.50	839.37	843.24
31,500	829.52	833.39	837.27	841.16	845.07	848.98	852.90	856.84
32,000	842.68	846.62	850.56	854.51	858.48	862.46	866.44	870.44
32,500	855.85	859.84	863.85	867.87	871.89	875.93	879.98	884.04
33,000	869.02	873.07	877.14	881.22	885.31	889.41	893.52	897.64
33,500	882.18	886.30	890.43	894.57	898.72	902.88	907.06	911.24
34,000	895.35	899.53	903.72	907.92	912.13	916.36	920.59	924.84
34,500	908.52	912.76	917.01	921.27	925.55	929.84	934.13	938.44
35,000	921.68	925.99	930.30	934.63	938.96	943.31	947.67	952.04

MONTHLY PAYMENTS FOR 60-MONTH CONVENTIONAL LOANS

Loan Amt.	8.00%	8.25%	8.50%	8.75%	9.00%	9.25%	9.50%	9.75%
$ 500	10.14	10.20	10.26	10.32	10.38	10.44	10.50	10.56
1,000	20.28	20.40	20.52	20.64	20.76	20.88	21.00	21.12
1,500	30.41	30.59	30.77	30.96	31.14	31.32	31.50	31.69
2,000	40.55	40.79	41.03	41.27	41.52	41.76	42.00	42.25
2,500	50.69	50.99	51.29	51.59	51.90	52.20	52.50	52.81
3,000	60.83	61.19	61.55	61.91	62.28	62.64	63.01	63.37
3,500	70.97	71.39	71.81	72.23	72.65	73.08	73.51	73.93
4,000	81.11	81.59	82.07	82.55	83.03	83.52	84.01	84.50
4,500	91.24	91.78	92.32	92.87	93.41	93.96	94.51	95.06
5,000	101.38	101.98	102.58	103.19	103.79	104.40	105.01	105.62
5,500	111.52	112.18	112.84	113.50	114.17	114.84	115.51	116.18
6,000	121.66	122.38	123.10	123.82	124.55	125.28	126.01	126.75
6,500	131.80	132.58	133.36	134.14	134.93	135.72	136.51	137.31
7,000	141.93	142.77	143.62	144.46	145.31	146.16	147.01	147.87
7,500	152.07	152.97	153.87	154.78	155.69	156.60	157.51	158.43
8,000	162.21	163.17	164.13	165.10	166.07	167.04	168.01	168.99
8,500	172.35	173.37	174.39	175.42	176.45	177.48	178.52	179.56
9,000	182.49	183.57	184.65	185.74	186.83	187.92	189.02	190.12
9,500	192.63	193.76	194.91	196.05	197.20	198.36	199.52	200.68
10,000	202.76	203.96	205.17	206.37	207.58	208.80	210.02	211.24
10,500	212.90	214.16	215.42	216.69	217.96	219.24	220.52	221.80
11,000	223.04	224.36	225.68	227.01	228.34	229.68	231.02	232.37
11,500	233.18	234.56	235.94	237.33	238.72	240.12	241.52	242.93
12,000	243.32	244.76	246.20	247.65	249.10	250.56	252.02	253.49
12,500	253.45	254.95	256.46	257.97	259.48	261.00	262.52	264.05
13,000	263.59	265.15	266.71	268.28	269.86	271.44	273.02	274.62
13,500	273.73	275.35	276.97	278.60	280.24	281.88	283.53	285.18
14,000	283.87	285.55	287.23	288.92	290.62	292.32	294.03	295.74
14,500	294.01	295.75	297.49	299.24	301.00	302.76	304.53	306.30
15,000	304.15	305.94	307.75	309.56	311.38	313.20	315.03	316.86
15,500	314.28	316.14	318.01	319.88	321.75	323.64	325.53	327.43
16,000	324.42	326.34	328.26	330.20	332.13	334.08	336.03	337.99
16,500	334.56	336.54	338.52	340.51	342.51	344.52	346.53	348.55
17,000	344.70	346.74	348.78	350.83	352.89	354.96	357.03	359.11
17,500	354.84	356.93	359.04	361.15	363.27	365.40	367.53	369.67
18,000	364.98	367.13	369.30	371.47	373.65	375.84	378.03	380.24
18,500	375.11	377.33	379.56	381.79	384.03	386.28	388.53	390.80
19,000	385.25	387.53	389.81	392.11	394.41	396.72	399.04	401.36
19,500	395.39	397.73	400.07	402.43	404.79	407.16	409.54	411.92
20,000	405.53	407.93	410.33	412.74	415.17	417.60	420.04	422.48
20,500	415.67	418.12	420.59	423.06	425.55	428.04	430.54	433.05
21,000	425.80	428.32	430.85	433.38	435.93	438.48	441.04	443.61
21,500	435.94	438.52	441.11	443.70	446.30	448.92	451.54	454.17
22,000	446.08	448.72	451.36	454.02	456.68	459.36	462.04	464.73
22,500	456.22	458.92	461.62	464.34	467.06	469.80	472.54	475.30
23,000	466.36	469.11	471.88	474.66	477.44	480.24	483.04	485.86
23,500	476.50	479.31	482.14	484.97	487.82	490.68	493.54	496.42
24,000	486.63	489.51	492.40	495.29	498.20	501.12	504.04	506.98
24,500	496.77	499.71	502.66	505.61	508.58	511.56	514.55	517.54
25,000	506.91	509.91	512.91	515.93	518.96	522.00	525.05	528.11
25,500	517.05	520.10	523.17	526.25	529.34	532.44	535.55	538.67
26,000	527.19	530.30	533.43	536.57	539.72	542.88	546.05	549.23
26,500	537.32	540.50	543.69	546.89	550.10	553.32	556.55	559.79
27,000	547.46	550.70	553.95	557.21	560.48	563.76	567.05	570.35
27,500	557.60	560.90	564.20	567.52	570.85	574.20	577.55	580.92
28,000	567.74	571.10	574.46	577.84	581.23	584.64	588.05	591.48
28,500	577.88	581.29	584.72	588.16	591.61	595.08	598.55	602.04
29,000	588.02	591.49	594.98	598.48	601.99	605.52	609.05	612.60
29,500	598.15	601.69	605.24	608.80	612.37	615.96	619.55	623.17
30,000	608.29	611.89	615.50	619.12	622.75	626.40	630.06	633.73
30,500	618.43	622.09	625.75	629.44	633.13	636.84	640.56	644.29
31,000	628.57	632.28	636.01	639.75	643.51	647.28	651.06	654.85
31,500	638.71	642.48	646.27	650.07	653.89	657.72	661.56	665.41
32,000	648.84	652.68	656.53	660.39	664.27	668.16	672.06	675.98
32,500	658.98	662.88	666.79	670.71	674.65	678.60	682.56	686.54
33,000	669.12	673.08	677.05	681.03	685.03	689.04	693.06	697.10
33,500	679.26	683.27	687.30	691.35	695.40	699.48	703.56	707.66
34,000	689.40	693.47	697.56	701.67	705.78	709.92	714.06	718.22
34,500	699.54	703.67	707.82	711.98	716.16	720.36	724.56	728.79
35,000	709.67	713.87	718.08	722.30	726.54	730.80	735.07	739.35

MONTHLY PAYMENTS FOR 60-MONTH CONVENTIONAL LOANS

Loan Amt.	10.00%	10.25%	10.50%	10.75%	11.00%	11.25%	11.50%	11.75%
$ 500	10.62	10.69	10.75	10.81	10.87	10.93	11.00	11.06
1,000	21.25	21.37	21.49	21.62	21.74	21.87	21.99	22.12
1,500	31.87	32.06	32.24	32.43	32.61	32.80	32.99	33.18
2,000	42.49	42.74	42.99	43.24	43.48	43.73	43.99	44.24
2,500	53.12	53.43	53.73	54.04	54.36	54.67	54.98	55.30
3,000	63.74	64.11	64.48	64.85	65.23	65.60	65.98	66.35
3,500	74.36	74.80	75.23	75.66	76.10	76.54	76.97	77.41
4,000	84.99	85.48	85.98	86.47	86.97	87.47	87.97	88.47
4,500	95.61	96.17	96.72	97.28	97.84	98.40	98.97	99.53
5,000	106.24	106.85	107.47	108.09	108.71	109.34	109.96	110.59
5,500	116.86	117.54	118.22	118.90	119.58	120.27	120.96	121.65
6,000	127.48	128.22	128.96	129.71	130.45	131.20	131.96	132.71
6,500	138.11	138.91	139.71	140.52	141.33	142.14	142.95	143.77
7,000	148.73	149.59	150.46	151.33	152.20	153.07	153.95	154.83
7,500	159.35	160.28	161.20	162.13	163.07	164.00	164.94	165.89
8,000	169.98	170.96	171.95	172.94	173.94	174.94	175.94	176.95
8,500	180.60	181.65	182.70	183.75	184.81	185.87	186.94	188.01
9,000	191.22	192.33	193.45	194.56	195.68	196.81	197.93	199.06
9,500	201.85	203.02	204.19	205.37	206.55	207.74	208.93	210.12
10,000	212.47	213.70	214.94	216.18	217.42	218.67	219.93	221.18
10,500	223.09	224.39	225.69	226.99	228.30	229.61	230.92	232.24
11,000	233.72	235.07	236.43	237.80	239.17	240.54	241.92	243.30
11,500	244.34	245.76	247.18	248.61	250.04	251.47	252.91	254.36
12,000	254.96	256.44	257.93	259.42	260.91	262.41	263.91	265.42
12,500	265.59	267.13	268.67	270.22	271.77	273.34	274.91	276.48
13,000	276.21	277.81	279.42	281.03	282.65	284.28	285.90	287.54
13,500	286.84	288.50	290.17	291.84	293.52	295.21	296.90	298.60
14,000	297.46	299.18	300.91	302.65	304.39	306.14	307.90	309.66
14,500	308.08	309.87	311.66	313.46	315.27	317.08	318.89	320.72
15,000	318.71	320.55	322.41	324.27	326.14	328.01	329.89	331.77
15,500	329.33	331.24	333.16	335.08	337.01	338.94	340.89	342.83
16,000	339.95	341.92	343.90	345.89	347.88	349.88	351.88	353.89
16,500	350.58	352.61	354.65	356.70	358.75	360.81	362.88	364.95
17,000	361.20	363.29	365.40	367.51	369.62	371.74	373.87	376.01
17,500	371.82	373.98	376.14	378.31	380.49	382.68	384.87	387.07
18,000	382.45	384.66	386.89	389.12	391.36	393.61	395.87	398.13
18,500	393.07	395.35	397.64	399.93	402.23	404.55	406.86	409.19
19,000	403.69	406.04	408.38	410.74	413.11	415.48	417.86	420.25
19,500	414.32	416.72	419.13	421.55	423.98	426.41	428.86	431.31
20,000	424.94	427.41	429.88	432.36	434.85	437.35	439.85	442.37
20,500	435.56	438.09	440.62	443.17	445.72	448.28	450.85	453.43
21,000	446.19	448.78	451.37	453.98	456.59	459.21	461.84	464.48
21,500	456.81	459.46	462.12	464.79	467.46	470.15	472.84	475.54
22,000	467.43	470.15	472.87	475.59	478.33	481.08	483.84	486.60
22,500	478.06	480.83	483.61	486.40	489.20	492.01	494.83	497.66
23,000	488.68	491.52	494.36	497.21	500.08	502.95	505.83	508.72
23,500	499.31	502.20	505.11	508.02	510.95	513.88	516.83	519.78
24,000	509.93	512.89	515.85	518.83	521.82	524.82	527.82	530.84
24,500	520.55	523.57	526.60	529.64	532.69	535.75	538.82	541.90
25,000	531.18	534.26	537.35	540.45	543.56	546.68	549.82	552.96
25,500	541.80	544.94	548.09	551.26	554.43	557.62	560.81	564.02
26,000	552.42	555.63	558.84	562.07	565.30	568.55	571.81	575.08
26,500	563.05	566.31	569.59	572.88	576.17	579.48	582.80	586.14
27,000	573.67	577.00	580.34	583.68	587.05	590.42	593.80	597.19
27,500	584.29	587.68	591.08	594.49	597.92	601.35	604.80	608.25
28,000	594.92	598.37	601.83	605.30	608.79	612.28	615.79	619.31
28,500	605.54	609.05	612.58	616.11	619.66	623.22	626.79	630.37
29,000	616.16	619.74	623.32	626.92	630.53	634.15	637.79	641.43
29,500	626.79	630.42	634.07	637.73	641.40	645.09	648.78	652.49
30,000	637.41	641.11	644.82	648.54	652.27	656.02	659.78	663.55
30,500	648.03	651.79	655.56	659.35	663.14	666.95	670.77	674.61
31,000	658.66	662.48	666.31	670.16	674.02	677.89	681.77	685.67
31,500	669.28	673.16	677.06	680.97	684.89	688.82	692.77	696.73
32,000	679.91	683.85	687.80	691.77	695.76	699.75	703.76	707.79
32,500	690.53	694.53	698.55	702.58	706.63	710.69	714.76	718.85
33,000	701.15	705.22	709.30	713.39	717.50	721.62	725.76	729.90
33,500	711.78	715.90	720.05	724.20	728.37	732.55	736.75	740.96
34,000	722.40	726.59	730.79	735.01	739.24	743.49	747.75	752.02
34,500	733.02	737.27	741.54	745.82	750.11	754.42	758.74	763.08
35,000	743.65	747.96	752.29	756.63	760.98	765.36	769.74	774.14

MONTHLY PAYMENTS FOR 60-MONTH CONVENTIONAL LOANS

Loan Amt.	12.00%	12.25%	12.50%	12.75%	13.00%	13.25%	13.50%	13.75%
$ 500	11.12	11.19	11.25	11.31	11.38	11.44	11.50	11.57
1,000	22.24	22.37	22.50	22.63	22.75	22.88	23.01	23.14
1,500	33.37	33.56	33.75	33.94	34.13	34.32	34.51	34.71
2,000	44.49	44.74	45.00	45.25	45.51	45.76	46.02	46.28
2,500	55.61	55.93	56.24	56.56	56.88	57.20	57.52	57.85
3,000	66.73	67.11	67.49	67.88	68.26	68.64	69.03	69.42
3,500	77.86	78.30	78.74	79.19	79.64	80.08	80.53	80.99
4,000	88.98	89.48	89.99	90.50	91.01	91.53	92.04	92.56
4,500	100.10	100.67	101.24	101.81	102.39	102.97	103.54	104.12
5,000	111.22	111.85	112.49	113.13	113.77	114.41	115.05	115.69
5,500	122.34	123.04	123.74	124.44	125.14	125.85	126.55	127.26
6,000	133.47	134.23	134.99	135.75	136.52	137.29	138.06	138.83
6,500	144.59	145.41	146.24	147.06	147.89	148.73	149.56	150.40
7,000	155.71	156.60	157.49	158.38	159.27	160.17	161.07	161.97
7,500	166.83	167.78	168.73	169.69	170.65	171.61	172.57	173.54
8,000	177.96	178.97	179.98	181.00	182.02	183.05	184.08	185.11
8,500	189.08	190.15	191.23	192.32	193.40	194.49	195.58	196.68
9,000	200.20	201.34	202.48	203.63	204.78	205.93	207.09	208.25
9,500	211.32	212.52	213.73	214.94	216.15	217.37	218.59	219.82
10,000	222.44	223.71	224.98	226.25	227.53	228.81	230.10	231.39
10,500	233.57	234.90	236.23	237.57	238.91	240.25	241.60	242.96
11,000	244.69	246.08	247.48	248.88	250.28	251.69	253.11	254.53
11,500	255.81	257.27	258.73	260.19	261.66	263.13	264.61	266.10
12,000	266.93	268.45	269.98	271.50	273.04	274.58	276.12	277.67
12,500	278.06	279.64	281.22	282.82	284.41	286.02	287.62	289.24
13,000	289.18	290.82	292.47	294.13	295.79	297.46	299.13	300.80
13,500	300.30	302.01	303.72	305.44	307.17	308.90	310.63	312.37
14,000	311.42	313.19	314.97	316.75	318.54	320.34	322.14	323.94
14,500	322.54	324.38	326.22	328.07	329.92	331.78	333.64	335.51
15,000	333.67	335.56	337.47	339.38	341.30	343.22	345.15	347.08
15,500	344.79	346.75	348.72	350.69	352.67	354.66	356.65	358.65
16,000	355.91	357.94	359.97	362.00	364.05	366.10	368.16	370.22
16,500	367.03	369.12	371.22	373.32	375.43	377.54	379.66	381.79
17,000	378.16	380.31	382.46	384.63	386.80	388.98	391.17	393.36
17,500	389.28	391.49	393.71	395.94	398.18	400.42	402.67	404.93
18,000	400.40	402.68	404.96	407.26	409.56	411.86	414.18	416.50
18,500	411.52	413.86	416.21	418.57	420.93	423.30	425.68	428.07
19,000	422.64	425.05	427.46	429.88	432.31	434.74	437.19	439.64
19,500	433.77	436.23	438.71	441.19	443.68	446.18	448.69	451.21
20,000	444.89	447.42	449.96	452.51	455.06	457.63	460.20	462.78
20,500	456.01	458.61	461.21	463.82	466.44	469.07	471.70	474.35
21,000	467.13	469.79	472.46	475.13	477.81	480.51	483.21	485.92
21,500	478.26	480.98	483.71	486.44	489.19	491.95	494.71	497.49
22,000	489.38	492.16	494.95	497.76	500.57	503.39	506.22	509.05
22,500	500.50	503.35	506.20	509.07	511.94	514.83	517.72	520.62
23,000	511.62	514.53	517.45	520.38	523.32	526.27	529.23	532.19
23,500	522.74	525.72	528.70	531.69	534.70	537.71	540.73	543.76
24,000	533.87	536.90	539.95	543.01	546.07	549.15	552.24	555.33
24,500	544.99	548.09	551.20	554.32	557.45	560.59	563.74	566.90
25,000	556.11	559.27	562.45	565.63	568.83	572.03	575.25	578.47
25,500	567.23	570.46	573.70	576.95	580.20	583.47	586.75	590.04
26,000	578.36	581.65	584.95	588.26	591.58	594.91	598.26	601.61
26,500	589.48	592.83	596.20	599.57	602.96	606.35	609.76	613.18
27,000	600.60	604.02	607.44	610.88	614.33	617.79	621.27	624.75
27,500	611.72	615.20	618.69	622.20	625.71	629.23	632.77	636.32
28,000	622.84	626.39	629.94	633.51	637.09	640.68	644.28	647.89
28,500	633.97	637.57	641.19	644.82	648.46	652.12	655.78	659.46
29,000	645.09	648.76	652.44	656.13	659.84	663.56	667.29	671.03
29,500	656.21	659.94	663.69	667.45	671.22	675.00	678.79	682.60
30,000	667.33	671.13	674.94	678.76	682.59	686.44	690.30	694.17
30,500	678.46	682.32	686.19	690.07	693.97	697.88	701.80	705.73
31,000	689.58	693.50	697.44	701.38	705.35	709.32	713.31	717.30
31,500	700.70	704.69	708.69	712.70	716.72	720.76	724.81	728.87
32,000	711.82	715.87	719.93	724.01	728.10	732.20	736.32	740.44
32,500	722.94	727.06	731.18	735.32	739.47	743.64	747.82	752.01
33,000	734.07	738.24	742.43	746.63	750.85	755.08	759.32	763.58
33,500	745.19	749.43	753.68	757.95	762.23	766.52	770.83	775.15
34,000	756.31	760.61	764.93	769.26	773.60	777.96	782.33	786.72
34,500	767.43	771.80	776.18	780.57	784.98	789.40	793.84	798.29
35,000	778.56	782.98	787.43	791.89	796.36	800.84	805.34	809.86

Index

Accidents, and termination liabilities, 65
Advertised deals, 39–40, 78–79
ALG leases, 46, 80, 82
ALG Residual Percentage Guide, 82
   cost of leasing, 33–38
   and long-term lease, 10
APR (annual percentage rate), 82. *See also* Finance charges; Interest rate
Assumption of lease. *See* Lease assumption
Auto dealership. *See* Dealership; Lessor

Bait-and-switch tactics, 41
Balloon payments, leasing to buy, 28, 82
Bank fee (sign-up fee), and cost of leasing, 35, 38
Banks. *See also* Lessors
   and cost of leasing, 33–38
   in manufacturer's leases, 18
   selling a leased car, 73
Better Business Bureau, and dealership reputation, 50
Bump, in price, 41, 43
Business use of vehicle, 23–28
Buyout. *See* Purchase option; Termination, early

Capital cost. *See* Manufacturer's suggested retail price; Principal

Capital cost depreciator (reducer). *See* Down payment
Cash flow, in leasing vs. purchase, 4–5
Cash reduction. *See* Down payment
Closed-end leases, 82
   compared to open-end, 2–3
   in leasing to buy, 28
   and termination, 64–65
Closer, 42
Consumer laws, and sales tactics, 44
Contract, 50–59
Corporate leasing, 51
Credit approval
   lease benefits quiz, 6–7
   in manufacturer's leases, 18

Damages. *See* Accidents; Depreciation; Wear and tear
Dealer costs. *See* Fees
Dealership. *See also* Lessor
   advantages in leasing, 76
   reputation, 50
   sales tactics, 38–44
   shopping for a lease, 33
Deductible, insurance, 60
Deductions, tax. *See* Tax deductions
Default, in contract specifications, 56
Depreciation, 82
   in closed- vs. open-end lease, 2–3
   and cost of leasing, 35
   and early termination, 66
   in high-mileage strategy, 20

in leasing vs. purchase, 5, 80
and termination, 65
Description, of vehicle, in
contract, 51
Destruction, in contract
specifications, 57–58,
60–61
Deterioration. *See* Accidents;
Depreciation; Wear and
tear
Down payment, 82
deceptive advertising, 39–40
in leasing to buy, 28, 29–30
in leasing vs. conventional
financing, 1–2, 4–5, 8,
29–30, 80
in manufacturer's leases, 17
reasons to lease, 75
shopping for a deal, 48
in short-term leases, 16

Early termination. *See*
Termination, early
Equity, 1–2, 83. *See also* Retail
equity; Wholesale equity
in long-term lease, 9, 10
Ethics, and sales tactics, 44
Excise tax, 55. *See also* Tax

Fair market value
in business leasing, 24
in high-mileage strategy, 20
purchase option, 70, 83
residuals, in conventional
purchase vs. leasing to
buy, 29
Fees, 2
contract specifications, 55
and purchase option, 70
shopping for a deal, 48

Finance charges, 2. *See also*
Interest rate
Fixed purchase option, 29, 83
Fraud, 38–45

Gap insurance, 61, 83
in short-term leases, 16

High-mileage strategy, 20–23
and long-term lease, 10
reasons to lease, 75
Highball tactic, 42–43
Hot buttons, 42

Inclusion amount, in business
leasing, 24
Income, 6–7
Inflation
in conventional purchase vs.
leasing to buy, 29–30, 80
in leasing to buy, 28
Initial charges
contract specifications, 54–55
shopping for a deal, 48
Insurance, 60–63
in business leasing, 27
contract specifications, 56,
79
gap. *See* Gap insurance
in short-term leases, 16
Interest rate
conventional financing vs.
leasing, 81
and cost of leasing, 34, 38
in long-term lease, 10
negotiating a lease, 78
Introductory offer, and
deceptive advertising, 40
Investment tax credit (ITC), 83
in long-term lease, 9

Law. *See* Consumer laws; Regulation M
Lease assumption, 82
　and early termination, 68
Level-yield interest, 84
Liability, in contract specifications, 53
Liability, insurance, 60
Licensing. *See* Fees
List price. *See* Manufacturer's suggested retail price
Long-term leases, 9–15, 84
　principal/payment ratio, 47
　vs. purchase, 9–13
Loss, in contract specifications, 57–58, 60–61
Lowball tactic, 41–42

Maintenance, 47
　business deductions, 28
　in high-mileage strategy, 23
Manufacturer's leases, 17–19, 84
　conventional purchase vs. leasing to buy, 29
　and early termination, 67
　and insurance, 61
Manufacturer's suggested retail price, 84. *See also* Price
　in business leasing, 24
　calculating lease payments, 79–80
　and cost of leasing, 33–38
　and highball tactic, 43
Market value. *See* Residual value; Equity
Mileage, 2, 8, 83
　contract specifications, 52
　in closed- vs. open-end lease, 2–3
　in high-mileage strategy, 20–23
　leasing vs. purchase costs, 6
　in long-term lease, 10
　and purchase option, 69–70
　reasons to lease, 75
　selling a leased car, 72
Money factor rate, and cost of leasing, 34–36
Monthly payment, 2
　contract specifications, 55
　conventional purchase vs. leasing to buy, 29, 30
　and cost of leasing, 36
　and early termination, 67
　and highball tactic, 43
　in long-term lease, 9–10
　vs. principal, 47
　in short-term leases, 16
　24-month conventional loan, 86–88
　36-month conventional loan, 89–91
　48-month conventional loan, 92–94
　60-month conventional loan, 95–97
MSRP. *See* Manufacturer's suggested retail price

NADA, 84
　residual value estimates, 13
NADA retail guide
　long-term vs. conventional lease, 13
　selling a leased car, 72
National Auto Dealers Association. *See* NADA
New Jersey, and cost of leasing, 36–37

Newspaper advertising, selling a leased car, 72
1986 tax program, and long-term lease, 9

Open-end leases, 84
  compared to closed-end, 2-3
  deceptive advertising, 40
  in leasing to buy, 28
  and Regulation M, 58
  and termination, 64, 70
Opportunity cost of money, 76
  in leasing to buy, 30
  in leasing vs. purchase, 4-5, 80
Option to buy. See Termination
Over-residualization, in manufacturer's leases, 17
Ownership, compared to leasing, 1-2

Payment schedule. See Monthly payment
Penalties, for early termination, 10. See also Termination, early; Unearned interest
Personal property tax, 37-38, 55. See also Tax
Personal use, vs. business use of vehicle, 23, 26
Price, 77
  in negotiating a lease, 78
  shopping for a deal, 47
  selling a leased car, 72
Principal, 82. See also Manufacturer's suggested retail price
  and cost of leasing, 35
  in long-term lease, 10
  vs. monthly payment, 47

Professional leasing, 51
Property tax. See Personal property tax
Purchase, vs. long-term lease, 9-13
Purchase option, 69-71, 82. See also Termination
  in contract, 51-52

Reconditioning charges, 64-65
  in high-mileage strategy, 23
Registration. See Fees
Regulation M, 50-51, 58, 84
  contract termination specifications, 54
  and purchase option, 70
  and termination, 64
Repairs
  contract specifications, 53
  selling a leased car, 72
  and termination, 65
Resale
  in leasing vs. purchase, 5
  and taxes, 12
Resale value. See Residual value
Residual value, 77, 84
  calculating lease payments, 79-80
  in closed- vs. open-end lease, 2-3
  in contract, 51-52
  and cost of leasing, 33-38
  and early termination, 67
  in high-mileage strategy, 20, 21
  and insurance, 61
  in long-term lease, 9, 10, 13
  in manufacturer's leases, 17
  negotiating a lease, 49, 78

and purchase option, 7–8, 28, 69–70
purchasing vs. leasing, 5, 29–31, 75, 80
selling a leased car, 73
Retail equity, 14. *See also* Equity
Retail value, vs. residual value, in long-term lease, 13
Risk, in closed- vs. open-end lease, 2–3
Rolling over
and early termination, 67
and insurance, 61–62

Sales tactics, 33, 38–45
Sales tax, 8
and cost of leasing, 36
in leasing vs. purchase, 4, 5, 29
in resale, 12
shopping for a deal, 48
Security deposit, 1–2, 84
contract specifications, 55
selling a leased car, 73
shopping for a deal, 48, 49
and termination, 64–65
Selling a leased car, 71–74
and early termination, 68–69
Service, as part of lease contract, 79
Short-term leasing, 15–16, 84
in high-mileage strategy, 20
payment/principal ratio, 47
Sign-up fee (bank fee), and cost of leasing, 35, 84
Springing the trade, and highball tactic, 43

Subleasing, 84–85
and early termination, 67
Substitute collateral, 85
and insurance, 62

Tax, 48, 70. *See also* Excise tax; Personal Property tax; Sales tax; Tax deductions
Tax deductions, 81
in business use of vehicle, 23–28
in leasing vs. purchase, 5
Termination, 6–8, 64–74. *See also* Purchase option
contract specifications, 52, 57
in leasing to buy, 28–32
in long-term lease, 10, 13
in manufacturer's leases, 17
Termination, early, 66–69, 83. *See also* Purchase option
contract specifications, 54
and insurance, 60–61
in long-term lease, 10
purchasing vs. leasing, 80
in short-term leases, 16
Termination fee, 70
Theft, in contract specifications, 57–58, 60–61
Title, selling a leased car, 73
Trade-in
and highball tactic, 43
in leasing vs. purchase, 4–5
Truth-in-Lending Act, 50–51

Unearned interest, 10, 80
Up-front costs. *See* Initial charges

Value. *See* Residual value; Price
Vehicle identification number, in contract, 51

Wear and tear
 in closed- vs. open-end lease, 2–3
 contract specifications, 52
 in high-mileage strategy, 23
 lease benefits quiz, 6–7
 in long-term vs. conventional lease, 13
 and termination, 65
Wholesale equity. *See also* Equity
 long-term lease example, 14
 selling a leased car, 73
Wholesale value, in manufacturer's leases, 17

Yield percentage rate, 85

```
                        5/91              90-1967
                                          92 A
388.32
S       Stewart, Gregory
              Smart guide to auto leasing.    1990
         $8




          1. Automobiles, Rental        0809241102
```